BUILDING
GOD'S HOUSE,

ONE STONE AT A TIME

Kent Evans

DEDICATION

To all the pastors, church leaders, prayer warriors, and those who faithfully and tirelessly work in their God-assigned places on the wall, for it is to you whom the Master was referring when He said, "Blessed is that servant, whom his lord when he cometh shall find so doing"
(Matt. 24:46).

To my family, Martha, April, Manuel, Courtney, Christian, Priscilla, Micaiah, Allaughna, Zion, Mikalya, Manuel IV, Giovanni, and Caleb, your love and support inspires and encourages me to continue to step out in faith to do God's will.

ACKNOWLEDGEMENTS

First of all, I thank the Spirit of God, my Teacher, for the inspiration to write and for teaching me "precept upon precept; line upon line" over the span of this book (Isa. 28:13).

I thank my wonderful wife, Pastor Martha Evans, who encouraged me to believe in myself and have enough confidence to undertake such a project.

I want to especially thank my daughter, Courtney Maddox, who helped me get "Building God's House, One Stone at a Time" out of the "moth balls" with her tireless editing efforts. Not only was her editing skills invaluable to the project, but her encouragement to me was invaluable too. Courtney continued to believe and encourage me that the message of the book was still relevant for the Church today.

I also thank Angelique Clarke for her assistance with the book cover and Rochelle Greene for taking one last look at all the details.

I thank my mother-in-law, Evangelist Florine Jackson, for being a true example of a prayer warrior. Her word to me has always been, "Son, some things come out only through prayer and fasting." It is a legacy such as hers that I desire to pass on to the next generation through this book.

I would also like to thank my mom and dad in the Lord, the late Apostle Ronald Thomas and Pastor Marvenelle who took the time to acknowledge and nurture the gifts in me. Without the teachings of Apostle Thomas, I would not have been able to gain the valuable insights that are in this book.

And finally, to my momma and daddy, Vinson and Janice Evans, who have been so patient with me and have always been there for me constantly praying for me as I do the will of the Father.

CONTENTS

INTRODUCTION

One night, the Lord asked me if I would be willing to be a part of the work that He was doing at a particular church. I agreed. Earlier that same night, I had visited this church where a member had taken me on a tour of their remodeling project that was well underway. He also shared with me about the remaining phases of the project. In the natural, I was quite impressed with how the new colors of carpet and baptistery drapes made the building look, but on the inside of me I was disturbed about the spiritual condition of that body of believers. After all, the people make up the church not the pews and the carpet. The Lord showed me a vision of what He saw when He looked at that church. I saw the same location with the building in ruins and the people walking around in the cold with no clothing to protect themselves from the elements. The Lord referred me to a passage of scripture to explain the vision.

> *And Jesus went out, and departed from the temple: and his disciples came to him for to show him the buildings of the temple. And Jesus said unto them, See ye not all these things? verily I say unto you, There shall not be left here one stone upon another, that shall not be thrown down.*
> *Matthew 24:1-2*

In this passage, the disciples were caught up in the beauty of the building, but Jesus didn't share their excitement. The Lord keyed in on this sentence when explaining the vision to me: "There shall not be one stone left upon another, that shall not be thrown down." He further explained to me that the spiritual condition of the church He was assigning me to was much like the one He prophesied about in this passage of scripture. None of the stones were joined together. You have to really demolish a building in order to separate all the stones from each other. Normally, at least a section will remain standing, but every stone was disconnected. I knew the condition of the church was bad, but it was not until four months later when God moved me to that church that I began to understand the significance of what He had said to me. We will discuss the vision in more detail later.

This church is not a rare case, but rather the norm for most churches. We in the Body of Christ seem to be majoring on the minors instead of the real important issues such as our relationship with God and our love for our fellow Christians. I write this book to the Body of Christ to stir the believers up to the greatest building project ever, building God's House. You can call me a modern day Nehemiah if you will. Nehemiah heard of the condition of the walls of Jerusalem as he and his people were in exile in a faraway land. The Spirit of the Lord stirred him up first of all to intercede for his people and then to lead them in a massive rebuilding project. The Lord is calling His people today to build His House, and in many cases He is calling us to rebuild His House. We could use another analogy here to describe the move of God at hand, getting the Church ready for the return of the Lord Jesus Christ. Jesus is soon to return, and the Word lets us know that He is coming for a glorious church without spot or wrinkle.

INTRODUCTION

Husbands, love your wives, even as Christ also loved the church, and gave himself for it; That he might sanctify and cleanse it with the washing of water by the word, That he might present it to himself a glorious church, not having spot, or wrinkle, or any such thing; but that it should be holy and without blemish. Ephesians 5:25-27

One day, I thought I was doing God a big favor by worrying about how the Church would ever get ready for His return. He spoke in my spirit the answer, "with the washing of water by the word." Notice that in verse 26 the washing of the water of the Word precedes the presentation of the bride to the groom. We must be ready in order to meet the groom. The preaching and teaching of the unadulterated Word will get the Body of Christ ready for the return of Jesus. The Word will always get the job done if we will just put the Word to work. Jesus is not coming back for a messed up house. Is your house in order? If not, you better get it ready and don't delay, for we do not know the day or the hour of His return.

CHAPTER 1

GOD'S BUILDING PROJECT

In the vision of the demolished church building, the Lord was showing me the spiritual condition of the church He was assigning me to. This church had everything going for them naturally speaking (a large budget, good attendance, a nice building, and a remodeling plan well underway), but spiritually speaking they were in sad shape. It was characterized by dead church services, no love for one another, a split right down the middle, and a pastor that was about ready to throw up his hands and quit. In this section, we will explore the significance of the stones in the reference scripture and the fact that none of these stones were connected together (Matt. 24:2).

Most Christians are still under the Old Testament thinking when it comes to the House of God. I have heard people refer to the church building as the House of God in their prayers. When I was a little boy people would say to me, "No running in the House of God." I grew up thinking that the church building was the House of God. Let's look at some scriptures to see what the Bible say about the House of God.

Who found favour before God, and desired to find a tabernacle for the God of Jacob. But Solomon built him an house. Howbeit the most High dwelleth not in temples made with hands; as saith the prophet, Heaven is my throne, and earth is my footstool: what house will ye build me? saith the Lord: or what is the place of my rest? Hath not my hand made all these things? Acts 7:46-50

Thus saith the LORD, The heaven is my throne, and the earth is my footstool: where is the house that ye build unto me? and where is the place of my rest? For all those things hath mine hand made, and all those things have been, saith the LORD: but to this man will I look, even to him that is poor and of a contrite spirit, and trembleth at my word. Isaiah 66:1-2

It is very clear that God never has and never will dwell in a temple made with hands. It couldn't contain Him anyway. God wants a heart just like the one described in Isaiah 66:2 to dwell in, "even to him that is poor and of a contrite spirit, and trembleth at my word." God wants to dwell in man. Again in I Corinthians 3:16, the Bible makes it very clear that we who have been born again are the temple of the Holy Spirit, not the church building.

Let's look at another passage that explains the House that God is building.

To whom coming, as unto a living stone, disallowed indeed of men, but chosen of God, and precious, Ye also, as lively stones, are built up a spiritual house, an holy priesthood, to offer up spiritual sacrifices, acceptable to God by Jesus Christ. Wherefore also it is contained in the scripture, Behold, I lay in Sion a chief corner stone, elect, precious: and he that believeth on him shall not be confounded. 1 Peter 2:4-6

We see that Jesus is the Chief Corner Stone, the first and the most important stone of the whole house, but notice also that we believers are living stones too. The plan of God is not to have a heap of stones just lying around, but we as living stones are to be BUILT UP into a spiritual house. This spiritual house is not for looks, but just as any other house, it is to keep something in as well as to keep something out. We are to be a holy priesthood offering up spiritual sacrifices that are acceptable to God.

> **A house is built to keep something in as well as to keep something out.**

Let's look at Ephesians 2:19-22 to get a better understanding.

> *Now therefore ye are no more strangers and foreigners, but fellow citizens with the saints, and of the household of God; And are built upon the foundation of the apostles and prophets, Jesus Christ himself being the chief corner stone; In whom all the building fitly framed together groweth unto an holy temple in the Lord: In whom ye also are builded together for an habitation of God through the Spirit. Ephesians 2:19-22*

Again, we see the Church being built upon this foundation laid by the apostles and the prophets with Jesus being the chief corner stone. Verse 22 even gives the purpose of this spiritual house, "AN HABITATION OF GOD THROUGH THE SPIRIT." Isn't that amazing! God wants us to come together so He can come in, hang out with us, and make us His home to dwell in. I don't know about you, but I like to be in services where God comes in and takes over. So many times we "have church" and that's about the extent of it. We sing a few songs, we hear a sermon, and we go home the same way we came. That's not what God intends for our services to be like.

In describing the order of service in the future temple that the children of Israel were to rebuild, God tells Ezekiel how we are supposed to leave.

> *But when the people of the land shall come before the LORD in the solemn feasts, he that entereth in by the way of the north gate to worship shall go out by the way of the south gate; and he that entereth by the way of the south gate shall go forth by the way of the north gate: he shall not return by the way of the gate whereby he came in, but shall go forth over against it. Ezekiel 46:9*

God never wants us to leave church the same way we came. As a matter of fact, when we get in the presence of God, you will never leave the same way you came. If you come to church sick, you should leave healed. If you come in burdened down, you should leave lifted up. If you come to church lost, you should leave saved. Do you get the idea? God wants to bless you, but we have to get God back into our services. Let's find out how to get Him back into our services and into His House.

CHAPTER 2

LOVE SETS THE STAGE FOR THE GLORY OF GOD

Let's take another look at Ephesians 2:19-22. Here we see that Jesus, the apostles, and the prophets laid the foundation for God's House. This foundation refers to the revelation and teachings of the New Testament Church. The Word of God is the foundation for God's House. We know from Jesus' teachings that if the foundation of any house is built on anything besides the rock, it will fall in the midst of the storms of life (Luke 6:49). A house must be built on the Word of God in order to withstand the attacks of hell. The Bible says that the Old Testament was written for our example. In Exodus, we find an example to understand the order of priority between the Word of God and love in order to usher the glory of God into His House.

> *And thou shalt put the mercy seat above upon the ark; and in the ark thou shalt put the testimony that I shall give thee. And there I will meet with thee, and I will commune with thee from above the mercy seat, from between the two cherubims which are upon the ark of the testimony, of all things which I will give thee in*

commandment unto the children of Israel.
Exodus 25:21-22

Notice the verse says, "And thou shalt put the mercy seat ABOVE upon the ark." Mercy must be placed above the Word, but the Word provides the foundation for mercy. If there was no ark that contained the Law, then the mercy seat could not be supported. Can you imagine the Word without mercy? That's a terrible thought. I don't know about you, but I need a lot of mercy.

Think for a minute about the operation of a two-cycle engine. In order for it to run smoothly and not incur permanent damage, you must get the right mix of gas and oil. The wrong mix will cause the engine to run as rough as a washboard. Just like the two-cycle engine with the wrong mix, a Christian with the improper balance of mercy and the Word can be dangerous and will soon find themselves in God's engine repair shop. If you ever run into a believer filled up with the Word and no mercy, they will bash you up side of the head with the Bible. They have knowledge of some select scriptures, but no compassion in their hearts. This is a perfect example of what the Bible means when it says, "the letter killeth, but the spirit giveth life" (II Cor. 3:6). Jesus was the Word made flesh (John 1:14), a walking Bible if you will (Heb.10:7), but compassion MOVED Him to the multitudes. When the written Word and the mercy of God were properly established, then the glory of God rested above the mercy seat. More than ever, the multitudes still need to be touched with the glory of God today.

> *Without a proper balance of mercy and the Word, one will soon find themselves in God's engine repair shop.*

In order to build, you must start with a good foundation, but there is more to a building than just the foundation. You can ride throughout a countryside and see many building projects with a foundation and a pile of blocks, but that doesn't make it a house. I have seen foundations and stacks of blocks just sit there with weeds growing around them, but it will never be a house until someone takes the blocks off of the pile, puts them on the foundation, and applies some cement. That describes the House of God today in many cases. We have all the right foundational teachings and bookstores full of "how to books," but no building is taking place. We must get the blocks off the pile, begin mixing the cement (the love of God), and place it between the blocks to get the House of God in progress.

> *And above all these things put on charity, which is the bond of perfectness. Colossians 3:14*

Love is the only thing that will bring us "lively stones" off of the pile, onto the wall, and cause us to be joined together.

> **Only God's love can bring the stones off the pile and form the perfect bond between them that keeps them together on the wall.**

I remember once, on my first assignment as a pastor, I took an elderly member to the hospital to see his wife. This feisty old fellow was a handful to say the least. Walking was quite a chore for him, and for him to sit required a doughnut-shaped cushion. After trying to persuade him for half an hour to let me take him home for the night, he talked me into letting him stay with his wife. When I left him and got in my car to go home, I discovered that he had left his cushion. After trying to convince myself that he probably wouldn't need it, I realized that this was hogwash. This man was dependent on that pillow, and I had better take a few minutes to treat him as I would want to be treated if I were in the same situation. Even though I had prayed for him and encouraged him to stand in faith for his healing, he still wanted his pillow. Regardless of how many scriptures I shared with him or how much faith I had for his healing, I couldn't make him receive his healing.

I was believing for his healing, but he was believing that God would ease his pain through the pain pills and the pillow. We were not in agreement. If I knew then what I know now, I would have first found out where his faith was and got in agreement with him. Jesus defined the prayer of agreement in Matt. 18:19: "if two of you shall AGREE on earth as touching any thing that they shall ask, it shall be done for them of my Father." Thank God I listened to the Holy Ghost and did the best thing I could have done in that situation, give this man his pillow. After handing over the pillow, he said, "Oh brother, love covers a multitude of sins, and you just covered a multitude of sins." Knowing this man's character, I realized that my kind deed had prevented a major scene.

At first, I thought his interpretation of the Scripture was way off. After further consideration, I realized that if we in the Body of Christ would do things for weaker Christians to help them avoid temptations, the devil wouldn't be near as successful in making people stumble and fall. The devil is always trying to offend baby Christians. We stronger Christians ought to "bear the infirmities of the weak, and not to please ourselves" (Rom.15:1). We should help them to shake the devil off, or better yet stop him before he gets his toe in the door. After all, the Bible says, "give the devil no place" (Eph. 4:27).

I don't know about you, but there have been times in my life when I was weak and really needed someone to stand with me. Once when I was heartbroken and confused over an experience, I couldn't figure out what my next step in life would be. I felt kind of like Elijah, having been used mightily by God one day and running scared at the death threats of Jezebel the next. I went to my friends for help, and all I got was a whole lot of do's and don'ts. I wanted someone to just listen and try to understand, but all I ran into were "speak the Word only" people. Don't get me wrong. I'm a faith person myself and have been guilty of the same thing at least a hundred times, but this time it felt a lot different because the shoe was on my foot. I'm merely illustrating the point that "faith worketh by love" and faith not motivated by love doesn't work or accomplish anything (Gal. 5:6).

I am thoroughly convinced that the reason Job's so called friends got into such hot water with God was because they beat Job over the head with the Word and didn't minister grace to him. Job didn't need a sermon at that time in his life. I am not saying that his confession was totally in line with what you or I may now understand from the New Testament when he said that "the thing that he greatly feared had come upon him" (Job 3:25). What I said was the man was going through a tragic time in his life to say the least. After all, the devil just wiped out his whole family. We usually think about his belongings, but having lost his wife and kids that had to have left him dumbfounded and distraught. I'm sure the last thing on your mind would be sheep and goats if you had just lost your family. To be real honest with you, a theological debate or even a genuine Bible study with friends was far from his mind at that moment. Job needed someone with a listening ear and a shoulder to cry on.

There is a time to correct a man, and there is a time just to listen and be there for him. You may think that you are so mighty in faith, but sometimes you will go through a season of sorrows.

> *Wherein ye greatly rejoice, though now for a season, if need be, ye are in heaviness through manifold temptations:*
> *1 Peter 1:6*

The Word says, "IF NEED BE." Sometimes you need to cry and get all that sorrow and grief out of your system. Don't try to be so tough that you keep it all in and explode. Contrary to what the world says, big boys do cry. Crying doesn't always mean you don't believe God; it simply shows emotions. We are not to judge and say if a person does or doesn't need to cry. Leave that up to them and God.

> *Job's so called friends got into trouble with God because they beat him up with the Word and did not minister grace to him.*

Notice that even though Job's confession was "wrong" according to some of today's faith teachers, God called him righteous before and after the test. Isn't that all that really matters? Dear friend you may have a head full of Bible knowledge, always confessing the right thing. You may have five different translations of the Bible plus the Greek and Hebrew dictionary, you may even be able to quote two thirds of the New Testament, but if you don't have love in your heart you won't make it into heaven. The Word is clear that there is only one indicator to show whether or not we have truly been saved: "We know that we have passed from death unto life, because we love the brethren" (I John 3:14).

Now as touching things offered unto idols, we know that we all have knowledge. Knowledge puffeth up, but charity edifieth. And if any man think that he knoweth any thing, he knoweth nothing yet as he ought to know. But if any man love God, the same is known of him.
1 Corinthians 8:1-3

You can find Amplified-toting, tongue-talking, Bible-thumping Christians, yea even ministers of the gospel that are rude and arrogant. My friend love is not rude and love is not boastful, arrogant, or inflated with pride. You may speak in tongues, prophesy, cast out devils, and do great and mighty things for God, but if you don't love God and do His will, Jesus said, on that day, He won't even know you (Matt. 7:21, 22). After all is said and done, to be known of God, like Job, is greater than anything else in this world. You can be broke, sick, and even mixed up in the head, but if your heart is in the right place with God, you can make it into heaven. Jesus even said you could go to heaven with one arm, or one foot, or even with one eye plucked out, but you can't make it in with sin in your heart (Matt. 18:8, 9). Jesus even instructed His disciples not to rejoice in their victories over the devil, but rejoice because their names are written in heaven (Luke 10:18-20). Don't be fooled by the devil. Don't major on your accomplishments or even on how much you know. You must always major on love, for God is Love. Then and only then will you be guaranteed success in life because "love never fails" (I Cor. 13:8).

> **When you think you are totally right, then God can no longer correct you.**

14

If you major on knowledge and getting your doctrines 100 percent right, you'll miss God every time. A minister was asked once why he was a part of a particular denomination. He replied, "Because I believe we are RIGHT." When I heard his answer, it struck me like a bad chord on a piano. That thought is so dangerous because when you think you are totally right, God can no longer correct you. That thought is the epitome of pride. Pride always wants to be right but never reconciled. Once another fellow, when comparing beliefs of two denominations, said, "So and so believes right like us." He then looked at me and asked, "We are right, ain't we?" Folks, if your church teaches you that they are RIGHT and that they have the whole counsel of God, then you need to find a church that has sense enough to admit that they don't have it all figured out. Thank God for what we do know, but on this side of heaven, at best, we only see through a glass dimly (I Cor. 13:12).

This leads me to the move that I believe is very crucial to the Body of Christ at this hour. There are large numbers of people in the Body of Christ that are thoroughly trained and skilled in the Word of God. They know the right scripture, the right confession, and the right prayer for every situation. Believe you me; they will correct you at the drop of a hat when you say the wrong thing. (I know, because God is still working on me.) We have to learn to love people into the Body of Christ, before we try to blow their doors off with the written Word. Dear saints, there are so many hurting people out there. Many are dazed and confused by the attacks of the enemy. There are racial and doctrinal divisions all throughout the Church. It is time for restoration. We need to build up our walls, and stop tearing them down. We need highly trained soldiers in the Word of God, motivated purely by God's love, whose sole purpose is to build and restore the Body of Christ.

Remember Nehemiah's dedication and how the enemy tried everything to stop him. What will it take to get you off the wall of restoration, to stop you from doing what God called you to do? Paul put it this way, "For I am persuaded, that (NOTHING) … shall be able to separate us from the love of God, which is in Christ Jesus our Lord" (Rom. 8:38-39). Notice he didn't say faith, he didn't say power, he didn't say miracles, but he did say LOVE. Why did he say love? Because God is love, and the love of God is what is going to get you into heaven. You have to keep yourself in the love of God by praying in the Holy Ghost (Jude 20). "And we know that all things work together for the good to them that LOVE God, to them who are the called according to HIS PURPOSE" (Rom. 8:28). What is your purpose? Your purpose is to build up the House of God. Your purpose is to speak the truth in LOVE so that others may grow thereby (Eph. 4:15). You may say, "Pastor Kent, I'm not a preacher or a teacher." We still have a call to walk in love and to let our light shine to those around us. The world will know that we are Christians by our LOVE (John 13:35). We need to tell the world about Jesus by living a life of love before them at work, at home, and everywhere we go.

> *You must use caution that your knowledge intake doesn't exceed your growth in love.*

Knowledge is so vital to the Body of Christ because without knowledge God's people are destroyed (Hos. 4:6). But there is a danger with knowledge also. Knowledge puffs up, but love edifies or builds up as we just read in I Corinthians 8:1. You must be careful that your knowledge intake doesn't exceed your love growth because it will puff you up.

And this I pray, that your love may abound yet more and more in knowledge and in all judgment; That ye may approve things that are excellent; that ye may be sincere and without offence till the day of Christ; Being filled with the fruits of righteousness, which are by Jesus Christ, unto the glory and praise of God. Philippians 1:9-11

This prayer will help you to get your perspective right and to grow in love. Notice the order set forth in this prayer. "And this I pray, that your love may abound yet more and more in Knowledge." Let your LOVE grow in knowledge. You can't separate the two, but the goal is that your love grows or abounds. Don't just get a bunch of knowledge without love. Get knowledge, but let it produce love in you. Then you will be a blessing to others. Then you will speak the truth in LOVE (not just to be heard) and cause people to GROW (Eph. 4:15).

CHAPTER 3

WATCHMEN ON THE WALLS

*But now I told them, "You know full well the tragedy of
our city; it lies in ruins and its gates are burned. Let us
rebuild the wall of Jerusalem and rid ourselves of this
disgrace!" Nehemiah 2:17 NLT*

In this verse, Nehemiah makes known his rebuilding plans to
the officials of Jerusalem. Notice he refers to the condition
of the city as a tragedy, and then he wants to rid the city of
"this DISGRACE." Now you may say, "Well that's no big deal to
have your walls broken and your gates burned." That is not the
way Nehemiah viewed it. He viewed it as a disgrace. The King
James Version reads: "let us build up the wall of Jerusalem, that
we be no more reproach." This lets us know that the enemies
were laughing at them. The enemy saw them as NO THREAT.
As a matter of fact, the enemies probably sat around and joked
about how easily they could go to the city and steal anything they
wanted. Thank God for Nehemiah. He said it was time to do
something about this DISGRACE. He was tired of the enemy
laughing at his people. It was time to start laughing at the enemy.

This report of the condition of Jerusalem lets us know
something else of great significance; there were no watchmen on

the walls because there were no walls. That was the clincher. There was no one to blow the trumpet in Zion. Danger could have been knocking at the door and no one would have even known it. It would kind of be like having a fire with no fire alarm. Danger is bad enough, but it is ten times worst with no warning. Can you imagine waking up in the middle of the night in your PJ's and having to fight the enemy? You need time to prepare if you are going to even stand a chance. Sneak attacks are the most deadly.

> *There can be no watchmen on the walls to protect and warn of coming dangers if there are no walls.*

Now, let's bring this example over into New Testament terminology and learn from it. I Corinthians 10:6 says the Old Testament was written for our example. In the New Testament, a watchman would be an intercessor, one that prays and warns others of danger. In Isaiah, we find an example of both good and bad watchmen. First, let's look at the good.

> *I have set watchmen upon thy walls, O Jerusalem, which shall never hold their peace day nor night: ye that make mention of the LORD, keep not silence, And give him no rest, till he establish, and till he make Jerusalem a praise in the earth.* Isaiah 62:6-7

These faithful watchmen are constantly before God's face reminding Him of His promises. If I want somebody to intercede for me, I sure want them to pray in line with God's Word. His Word is His will.

Now, let's look at the bad watchmen.

All ye beasts of the field, come to devour, yea, all ye beasts in the forest. His watchmen are blind: they are all ignorant, they are all dumb dogs, they cannot bark; sleeping, lying down, loving to slumber. Yea, they are greedy dogs which can never have enough, and they are shepherds that cannot understand: they all look to their own way, every one for his gain, from his quarter. Come ye, say they, I will fetch wine, and we will fill ourselves with strong drink; and to morrow shall be as this day, and much more abundant.   Isaiah 56:9-12

These watchmen had a poor track record. They were BLIND, IGNORANT, DUMB, DOGS THAT COULDN'T BARK, and LOVED TO SLUMBER. Their track record continues, but you get the picture. If I had a watchdog that couldn't bark, I would stop feeding it. A watchdog is no good if it can't bark.

> **A church with no walls is a church with no prayer. A church with no prayer is a church with no power.**

I remember once I was picking up something from a man's property when he wasn't home, and his dog just lay under an old pickup truck tied. I practically forgot about the dog. I could have taken anything I wanted, but when the man returned home the dog almost turned the truck over to get to me. He growled so that I thought I was going to jump out of my skin. It was useless to bark after the owner was already aware that I was there. That reminds me of a lot of churches today. The devil is sitting in church with them and they don't even recognize him, much less bark. You show me a church with no walls, or bonds, or ties with each other and, I'll show you a church with NO PRAYER. If you show me a church with no prayer, I'll show you

20

a church with NO POWER and a church with the devil running the show. Not only is a watchman an intercessor, but a watchman can also be a prophet. Ezekiel was a prophet and God also called him to be a watchman over the house of Israel (Ezek. 3:17). Prophets are noted for their ability see. In Ezekiel's case, he saw the coming judgment, warned the nation of Israel, and urgently pled with them to change their course. This gift is essential for the Church to see the danger before it arrives and to be prepared for it.

As you read the first six chapters of Nehemiah you will find that the enemy thought that Jerusalem was no threat to them. All of a sudden, they began to take note when construction began. The enemy tried mocking, threatening, and discouraging Nehemiah and company to get them to stop building the walls, but when the enemy heard that there was NO BREACH in the wall, they got down and dirty. The enemy came and said, "Hey lets meet together and have a peace talk." They came not once, but four times to get Nehemiah to talk. The enemy couldn't get Nehemiah to stop building, so they started spreading lies about Nehemiah and his plans. Isn't that just like the devil? If he can't get you with a compromise, he will start spreading lies about you.

You can be sold out and so on fire for Jesus that seemingly nothing could even touch you, but when the devil starts spreading lies about you, that can really throw you for a loop. If you don't remain rooted and grounded in the Word, the devil will have you chasing after those lies trying to straighten them out. That is exactly what the devil wants you to do, get off the wall. Let God defend you! The battle is not yours anyway; it's the Lord's. The truth will always win out in the end. Don't be moved by the devil's lies. The main point is that the enemy didn't get serious until he found out that there was NO BREACH. The devil knows that if he can keep us divided, we will fall, but if we unite together, then we will be able to stand against him. He also knows that every time we come together we are ten times stronger; therefore, the devil's number one tactic is to divide the church. He knows that "if a house be divided against itself, that house CANNOT STAND" (Mark 3:25).

> *The enemy did not view the people of God as a threat or even come after them until there was no breach in the wall.*

Now, let's look at one of the most powerful verses about intercessory prayer and judgment in the whole Bible.

> *I looked for someone who might rebuild the wall of righteousness that guards the land. I searched for someone to stand in the gap in the wall so I wouldn't have to destroy the land, but I found no one. Ezekiel 22:30 NLT*

Whereas Nehemiah wrote during the restoration period of Jerusalem, after the fall, Ezekiel wrote while he was in Babylonian captivity (Ezek. 1:1). Ezekiel sent numerous warnings to Jerusalem to urge them to repent to God and change their course to avoid the coming destruction. God spoke to Ezekiel the very same day that the king of Babylon set himself against the city of Jerusalem (Ezek. 24:1-2) and warned that He would take away the desire of Israel, the Temple which had become "the source of their security and pride" (Ezek. 24:21 NLT). God confirmed this through an object lesson that was very near and dear to the prophet's heart, the loss of his wife in which God told him not to show any sorrow (Ezek. 24:15-21). Later in chapter 33, Ezekiel received a report from a messenger that the city was "smitten," and on that very day, God opened the mouth of the prophet that had been shut since the beginning of his ministry as a sign to the rebellious house of Israel (Ezek. 3:26; 33:21).

BEFORE judgment is the time to intercede for mercy, for when judgment falls it is too late. Both Ezekiel and Nehemiah knew well what a breach in the wall meant. Ezekiel saw beforehand the enemy forces coming to seize the city of Jerusalem and destroy its walls; he knew that an intercessor was the only way to prevent the coming judgment. Nehemiah knew that the walls of defense had to be rebuilt in order to keep history from repeating itself.

With that setting in mind, let's break this verse down. First of all, God was looking for a man. Isn't that interesting? Before God gets ready to send judgment, He seeks out a man to pray for a nation that he might not destroy it. Now, that might blow your theology, but that is Bible just the same. What did God need this man to do? He needed this man to build up the wall and to stand in the gap for the nation. Now, in Ezekiel's day God didn't find that man. If He had, then Jerusalem could have been spared. That's amazing! God would have spared the whole nation if somebody would have "stood in places where the wall had crumbled and DEFEND the land" from God's fierce wrath (Ezek. 22:30 GNT). Notice from the New Living Translation above, that "wall of righteousness" was attributed to guarding the whole land, "build again the wall of righteousness that GUARDS THE LAND."

Remember the first examples of an intercessor in the Bible. Abraham stood in the gap for Sodom and Gomorrah. As Abraham pled his case with God, he did so on the basis of the number of righteous men in the nation. Abraham's plea went from 50 to 10 righteous men. The point is that God would have spared the whole nation if the righteous quorum was met. God obviously didn't find the number of righteous people in the cities of Sodom and Gomorrah, so He did the next best thing. He removed the righteous from the city before the judgment fell. The only reason we as a nation have been spared from destruction is because of the righteous men and women who have stood in the gap for this nation and because of the number of righteous people in the land, or the righteous quorum.

You might think that the number of F-16's and nuclear missiles is the key to our national security, but the Bible makes it clear that "except the Lord KEEP THE CITY, the watchman waketh but in vain" (Ps. 127:1). I believe Ruth Graham spoke one of the most profound statements concerning our nation that I have ever heard. She said, "If God doesn't punish America, He will have to apologize to Sodom and Gomorrah." That should remind us that God is keeping a close watch on the escalating sins and the many abominations committed in this nation. God is still on the throne, and He is "the Judge of all the earth" (Gen. 18:25). The lesson to be learned here is that we can turn that judgment around by our prayers if we start in time, but God will not let sin go unchecked indefinitely. We have such a powerful covenant with God, and so often we fail to realize just how powerful our prayers are.

> *It is not the Navy Destroyers and F16's that protect the land. It is the righteous who stand in the breach for the defense of the land.*

Instead of prayer, I hear so many Christians criticizing the president and our leaders. That lets me know that they are not praying for our country. We are called by God to speak out when our leaders govern contrary to the Word. Our job is to proclaim the truth at all times. We simply cannot agree with our leaders when they speak lies and even false doctrines. We are called to be salt and light, but at the same time, God never told us to judge or to be critical. Our job is to pray for our nation and those who have authority over us.

> *I exhort therefore, that, first of all, supplications, prayers, intercessions, and giving of thanks, be made for all men; For kings, and for all that are in authority; that we may lead a quiet and peaceable life in all godliness and honesty.*
> *1 Timothy 2:1-2*

Notice this verse didn't say anything about complaining how bad you think the president or congress is. It said pray for them "that we may lead a quiet and peaceable life." God placed the power in our hands to pray for our country, and He holds us responsible. Our prayers can change the course of this nation. Sad to say most Christians aren't praying for our country and its leaders. It is time for the Church to get on its knees and begin to pray that God's will be done. The Bible says that the king's heart is in God's hand, and He can turn the king's heart wherever He wishes (Prov. 21:1). We must pray boldly as a covenant person in right standing with God as Abraham did. Then and only then will we see our nation change.

Nehemiah is another prime example of what one man can do for a whole nation. Nehemiah 1:4 tells us that after hearing the news of Jerusalem's condition, Nehemiah "mourned certain days, and FASTED, and PRAYED before the God of heaven." It didn't say that he called a prayer meeting or even got another brother to be in agreement. The Word tells us that by Nehemiah's prayer and fasting alone God changed the course of Jerusalem's history. God restored that city and its walls, so that Jerusalem would once again have WATCHMEN ON ITS WALLS.

CHAPTER 4

UNITY

We Are One in the Spirit

We are one in the Spirit, we are one in the Lord.
We are one in the Spirit, we are one in the Lord.
And we pray that our unity may one day be restored.
And they'll know we are Christians by our love by our love.
Yes they'll know we are Christians by our love.
- Author Unknown

I remember very vividly singing that simple song in the youth choir at our church as a boy. I didn't realize the powerful message in that song at that time, *One in the Spirit*, as I do now. I have come to know and understand that unity is the greatest need in the Body of Christ at this hour. In Mark 3:25, Jesus made it plain and simple that the House of God, or any house for that matter, cannot stand if there is division in it. Your household will fall if you let division in. There is strength in numbers. Do you remember the tower of Babel? They were so united that God had to scramble their language to stop them. God said, "Behold the people is ONE, and they have all ONE language; and this they began to do: and now NOTHING will be restrained from them ..." (Gen. 11:6). This lets us know just how powerful we could be for God if we would simply unite together against the enemy.

> *How should one chase a thousand, and two put ten thousand to flight, except their Rock had sold them, and the LORD had shut them up? Deuteronomy 32:30*

We are ten times stronger every time two of us come together in the spirit. If we get a whole congregation to come together in true unity we could run every devil off for miles around. Revival would break out on every corner. All the juke joints would have to close down. The drug pushers would be put out of business. All the policemen could breathe a sigh of relief. The emergency rescue teams and ambulances could take a much needed rest. The devil is the source of all violence, hurt, harm and danger. Wouldn't that be such a pleasant change to turn on the news and hear the announcer say, "Well there is no bad news tonight; there is only good news." Folks, that sounds farfetched, but get ready because this is going to happen. The Glory of God is going to sweep this land and the news reporters are going to be so baffled they won't know what to do. Can you imagine the look on the news anchor person's face when he or she starts talking about stadiums filled with people getting saved, filled with the Holy Ghost, and healed to the glory of God? Now, do you get a taste of why we should endeavor to keep the unity?

> **We are ten times stronger every time two of us come together in the spirit.**

In understanding more about the power in unity, is it any small wonder why the devil's number one strategy is to keep the House of God divided? Nehemiah and company were fine as long as they sat around the camp fire singing, "How great Thou art" and testifying, but as soon as they picked up the first stone off the rubbish pile and started to rebuild the walls of Jerusalem, every devil from miles around came to discourage and threaten them. But, that didn't stop them from praising God; they kept right on building until the wall was complete.

When I began my first pastorate, I started to dig into the subject of division and unity. As I searched the scriptures, I became intrigued with this verse:

A wholesome tongue is a tree of life: but perverseness therein is a breach in the spirit. Proverbs 15:4

Although unsure of the meaning, I was drawn to the verse, and began to enquire of the Lord. One day, while I was eating lunch, down on the inside I heard the Holy Ghost say, "Breach in the spirit as opposed to unity in the spirit." I got it then! I knew then He was talking about a corporate thing and not an individual thing. If you get someone who's contrary and that sows discord among the brethren, then you will have a breach or a division in the spirit.

> **One with a contrary attitude in the church will cause a breach in the spirit or division.**

As I visited the members of that church, I noticed terms like "us" and "them" being used. Now in this church, everyone would speak to one another, do nice things for one another and all go to the church together, but there was no unity. Or I could say it this way, there was no coming together for a common cause. That is not to say that everybody was in chaos, but when the group that consisted of the leaders, or the "active members," would decide to do something, the other group, or the "non-active members," would drag their feet, murmur, and complain. Oh not complaining openly, but always behind the scene with gossip, backbiting, and murmuring. I remember one Sunday in the middle of the sermon, I asked, "Who in the world is 'us' and who is 'them' anyway? We are all one body anyway aren't we?" Although they did not seem to be moved by that profound statement, it opened my eyes to the fact that although we all sat under the same roof and were members of the same church, we were split right down the middle. Usually, every Sunday the "us's" sat to the right, and the "them's" sat to the left. I called it an invisible split right down the middle.

Referring back to Proverbs 15:4 notice that when "perverseness" is in the body, there is a "breach in the spirit." Perverseness is better explained in the dictionary as stubborn, contrary, or persisting in error. Have you ever seen anyone like that in your church? Have you ever tried to plan something for the whole church and everyone almost was in agreement except for a few that refused to go along with you? That's being contrary. I'm talking about petty stuff like planning where to have a picnic, not about a five million dollar building project. You know, just being down right contrary just to be contrary. We Christians need to stop being selfish and start being concerned with what is BEST FOR THE WHOLE BODY. Stop being LONE RANGERS and start being TEAM PLAYERS. The Word lets us know how to get rid of strife and contrariness. First, you must, "Cast out the scorner, and contention shall go out; yea, strife and reproach shall cease" (Prov. 22:10). Secondly, you must stop putting wood on the fire, for "Where no wood is, there the fire goeth out: so where there is no talebearer, the strife ceaseth. As coals are to burning coals, and wood to fire; so is a contentious man to kindle strife" (Prov. 26:20-21).

The Word is clear. In order to get rid of strife and contention in the body, we must get rid of all gossip, whispering, and talebearing. If you study Proverbs, you'll find that these words are used interchangeably. If you have the wrong kind of fire in your church, you must put it out. There is only one way to stop a fire; you must stop putting wood on it. James says it this way, "Behold how great matter a little fire kindleth! And the tongue is a FIRE, a world of iniquity" (James 3:5-6). Verse 6 goes on to say that the tongue, "setteth on FIRE the course of nature; and it is set on FIRE of HELL." First and foremost, hell, or the devil, wants to use your tongue to destroy your church by dissolving the strong bonds of love that keep the members together and make up the walls of protection. Secondly, he wants to destroy you. Get gossip and destructive talk out of your church and ALL strife will cease. Start speaking the TRUTH in LOVE and your church will GROW warm and close together again in LOVE. So let's get those gossip spirits out of the church and get united.

> *As Christians, we need to stop being selfish and start being team players that think of what is best for the whole body.*

CHAPTER 5

UNITED IN PRAYER

The biggest danger of gossip in the church is that it prevents us from praying as we should. The more you gossip the less you pray. The more you pray the less you gossip; it's just that simple. So, remember when you are tempted by the devil to gossip, you really should be praying that God's will would be done in that individual's life instead of the devil's. Think of it this way, you can pray for God's will to be done or you can gossip for the devil's will to be done. Have you ever heard of constructive gossip? Gossipers are the devil's intercessors. Whose side are you on? Next time you feel tempted to tear your brother or sister down, remember that you would in fact be tearing yourself down, for we all are members of the same body (I Cor. 12:27).

> *Prayer and gossip are inversely proportional – the more you gossip the less you pray, the more you pray the less you gossip.*

While studying on the subject of division, I noticed the real danger of gossip in the church. As prayer needs arose, I watched how others responded. Let's say for example Brother Joe has been tempted by the devil in the area of lust. Brother Joe decides that this attack is too much for his faith alone, so he goes to Brother Jim for help. If the truth be known, Brother Jim has been gossiping about Brother Joe and his slip ups to other members in the church. When Brother Jim is asked to pray, he must decide to do one of two things: "fess up" or either play act. He could say, "Hey Brother Joe I've been gossiping about you and not praying for you as I should." Or, he could lie and go along with Brother Joe as if his hypocritical prayer could do some good. If he so chose the first option, the two could experience reconciliation and the power of God would come on the scene as they agreed in prayer. Not only does gossip keep Joe and Jim from praying as they should, it separates them.

A froward man soweth strife: and a whisperer separateth chief friends. Proverbs 16:28

The good news is that if gossip can separate the best of friends, then prayer will keep them together or bring about unity.

I remember one Saturday night before I had to preach the next day; I had a very sharp pain in my eye that grew worse as the day went on. The pain had gotten to the point that my right eye was red and full of tears. My mind certainly was not on ministering the Word. I knew I had to get quiet before the Lord before I preached, but all I could do was focus on the intensity of the pain. Now, bear in mind that this took place while I was preaching on gossip at the small church where I pastored. As I lay down on my bed and just held my eye, the Holy Ghost came to the rescue as He always does. He brought to my attention an example Brother Derrick Prince gave on his tape entitled, *From Curses to Blessings.* Brother Prince was experiencing a sharp pain and the Lord showed Him that some people in his family were speaking against him. He followed the Lord's instructions and rolled back every soulish utterance and gossip in the name of Jesus. I immediately did the same thing. (It is amazing how agreeable you can be when you are in pain.) Within 30 seconds the pain behind my eye subsided. It was evident that gossip against me was the source of the affliction. I got right up from my bed and went and had supper with my family, praising God. After supper, I was able to get quiet before the Lord and prepare for the message for the next day.

Now, every pain in your head is not from gossip, but be aware that gossip can have a physical effect on you. Be aware also that you are being used by Satan for evil when you gossip and not for good. If you are open to Him, the Lord will show you what is going on.   Now, somebody from the church was probably expressing their disagreement or dislikes with their young preacher and slipped over into gossip. Satan was able to use this to launch an evil spirit against me to try to prevent the message to God's people. The real issue here is that if some church member would had have listened to the Holy Ghost and prayed to God to help their young pastor to hear from heaven and speak His Word, things could have been a lot different Sunday morning. Remember, your gossip could very well prevent some from getting saved if you hindered the man or woman of God from delivering the Word of God. Also remember, "Touch not mine anointed and do my prophets NO HARM" (I Chron. 16:22). In other words, if you want to avoid getting in trouble with God about His work, keep your lips off of other ministries and ministers.

> *You can aid the spreading of the gospel with your prayers, or you can also hinder it with your gossip.*

Gossip is simply a destructive conversation about someone else, and that's exactly what Satan uses witches to do. I heard a testimony of a real witch who had been converted to Christianity. She talked about how witches get together in their covens and constantly put curses on Christians such as sickness, disease, poverty, and death. That is a summary of Deuteronomy 28's list of curses! Satan doesn't care if you are a member of a witches coven or a member of the First Baptist Church. All he wants is your tongue. If he can get your tongue to speak out his ill wishes, then he can bring them to pass if he is not stopped.

Along the same lines, I had God to send me a brother to share a testimony that helped me to understand this subject more clearly. At the time, I was looking for a way out of giving a message at the Baptist Campus Ministry meeting about being filled with the Spirit with the evidence of speaking with other tongues (Acts 2:4). He came to me and said, "You tell the Baptist about being filled with the Holy Ghost. When I was in Africa, I was possessed with a devil. When a minister that was not filled with the Holy Ghost would tell me about Jesus, I would laugh in his face, but when a minister that was filled with the Holy Ghost would say the Name of Jesus, I saw fire in his eyes and I would fall to the ground." He also said that his grandfather, who was a witch doctor, said, "Don't put a curse on a tongue-talking Christian because they will put it back on you." This was a common quote among the witch doctors according to this brother from Africa.

You need to be filled with the Holy Ghost. Listen, the devil is not playing with his attacks on the saints. He knows that his time is short. He doesn't care if you are a witch doctor by name or not. All he really wants is your tongue and to fill your heart with hatred so that you will speak his ill-wishes against your brother or your sister. You may ask, "Can a Christian put a curse on someone?" Why most certainly! Look at this verse:

But the tongue can no man tame; it is an unruly evil, full of deadly poison. Therewith bless we God, even the Father; and therewith curse we men, which are made after the similitude of God. Out of the same mouth proceedeth blessing and cursing. My brethren, these things ought not so to be. James 3:8-10

Notice that the scripture says "out of the same mouth," and that "these things ought not so to be." You bless God out of one side of your mouth, and out of the other side of your mouth you curse men that are made in His image. We need to wake up in the Body of Christ and start walking in love with each other. We need to do our part to help our brothers and sisters by not speaking destruction upon them. It has been said that, "Christians are the only ones who bury their wounded." God's love in us should prevent us from doing that. We must speak the truth in love so that we may grow. We have life and death in the power of our tongues. We must stop speaking death to our brothers and sisters in Christ and start speaking life. In Galatians 6:1, the spiritual Christians are told to restore those that have been over taken in a fault with a spirit of meekness. If we are truly spiritual or mature Christians, we will restore one another and not tear down our own.

> **We must stop speaking death to our brothers and sisters ... if we are truly spiritual, we will restore one another and not tear down our own.**

When I began to study about unity and division, I noticed that when we really come together with one accord and pray, God's power will always show up. The following passages show the pattern by which the early church came together and experienced a mighty move of God's power.

And when the day of Pentecost was fully come, they were all with one accord in one place. And suddenly there came a sound from heaven as of a rushing mighty wind, and it filled all the house where they were sitting. And there appeared unto them cloven tongues like as of fire, and it sat upon each of them. And they were all filled with the Holy Ghost, and began to speak with other tongues, as the Spirit gave them utterance. Acts 2:1-4

And when they heard that, they lifted up their voice to God with one accord, and said, Lord, thou art God, which hast made heaven, and earth, and the sea, and all that in them is: Who by the mouth of thy servant David hast said, Why did the heathen rage, and the people imagine vain things? The kings of the earth stood up, and the rulers were gathered together against the Lord, and against his Christ. For of a truth against thy holy child Jesus, whom thou hast anointed, both Herod, and Pontius Pilate, with the Gentiles, and the people of Israel, were gathered together, For to do whatsoever thy hand and thy counsel determined before to be done. And now, Lord, behold their threatenings: and grant unto thy servants, that with all boldness they may speak thy word, By stretching forth thine hand to heal; and that signs and wonders may be done by the name of thy holy child Jesus. And when they had prayed, the place was shaken where they were assembled together; and they were all filled with the Holy Ghost, and they spake the Word of God with boldness. Acts 4:24-31

Notice how together they were. They were in ONE PLACE, with ONE VOICE, and with ONE ACCORD. The prayer described here is often referred to as the United Prayer. This prayer is vital in order for the Church to accomplish her assignment. When you get a group of people in one room and achieve one VOICE, you have reached unity, and God will shake your building and community with His awesome power.

> *The United Prayer is a powerful prayer that takes place when the Church is in one place, with one voice, and with one accord.*

I remember once while leading a Bible study and prayer, these scriptures about unity in prayer began to burn in my heart. The group I was leading, well let's just say they hadn't obtained that degree of unity yet. To be truthful, they were with NO ACCORD. One night I had a brain storm. Again Acts 2:1 says, "they were all with ONE ACCORD IN ONE PLACE." Typically on Wednesday nights the members would come in and scatter across the back of the church. I was set up with a podium at the front left. Before, I would have gone to the back where everybody was sitting to have prayer. This time I was enlightened by the scriptures, so I called them to the front around the altar. At least this time we were all in one place, but sad to say we were not WITH ONE ACCORD. I gave everybody a chance to pray first and then I was going to close out the time of prayer. The time of silence was almost unbearable. Three or four minutes seemed like an eternity. No one prayed except for one deacon. So, after waiting much more than sufficient time for everyone to have a chance to pray, I jumped in and tried to pray the power down. I came to the conclusion as my daddy always says, "You can lead a horse to water but you can't make him drink." The same is true in prayer and unity. You can get them all in one place, but you can't make them get with one accord. True oneness only comes when we began to make adjustments in our hearts and minds to come together as a group, for with one accord means with one mind, one purpose.

Paul writes to a group of Christians much like the group I just wrote about that was all fired up but not about the right thing. They were divided up about who baptized who or whose ministry was better than the other. It kind of sounded like people getting all fired up about which football team they liked the best. Some say, the Dallas Cowboys are the best, and others say Miami is the best. The point that I'm making is that type rivalry has no place in the Body of Christ. Comments like "Well if so and so ain't preaching tonight, I'm not going," or "Brother so and so is the greatest, nobody can preach like him," don't promote unity in the Body but rather division. Paul refers to this plain and simply as carnality (I Cor. 3:1).

Thank God for Paul and how God used him to SPEAK THE TRUTH IN LOVE to them. You and I would have written them off and called them bad names, but Paul was so positive, so constructive. Notice how he encourages them to pull together.

> *Now I beseech you, brethren, by the name of our Lord Jesus Christ, that ye all speak the same thing, and that there be no divisions among you; but that ye be perfectly joined together in the same mind and in the same judgment. For it hath been declared unto me of you, my brethren, by them which are of the house of Chloe, that there are contentions among you. 1 Corinthians 1:10-11*

The first line of verse 10 sounds like the verse we read in Acts 4:24 where they had one voice. Now, these believers by no means had one voice, but Paul through the Holy Ghost is telling them how to obtain unity. The same will work in our congregations. First, we must all speak the same thing. You can't be striving about which preacher you like the best or who baptized you. Paul said, "I thank God that I baptized none of you, but Crispus and Gaius lest any should say that I baptized in my own name" (I Cor. 1:14, 15). They were not all saying the same thing. They were all pulling different directions. Notice back in verse 10 of the same chapter, the way to eliminate division is to say the same thing. Now, I'm not talking about a bunch of robots walking around sounding like a broken record, but I'm talking about speaking the truth in love and causing people to grow. Speaking what the Bible says and leaving your opinions at home.

> *In order to be perfectly joined together, we must all speak the same thing and leave our opinions at home.*

In the 14th chapter of 1 Corinthians he wrote to the same bunch and told every one of them (not just a hand full of seasoned intercessors) to come together with a psalms, with a doctrine, a tongue, a revelation, or an interpretation. Sometime intercessors because of their keen sensitivity can be divisive too. They must stay focused and "stand in the gap" instead of gossiping about it. Intercessors must stay on the wall and not get sidetracked with talking about the problems of the congregation that the Lord shows them. At the end of verse 26 he said to "Let all things be done unto edifying." We are to minister GRACE to the hearers, helping people out and not putting them down. We are to "Pray without ceasing" (I Thess. 5:17). If we keep this attitude of prayer, we will not participate in gossip and destructive conversation. That's what the Word of God is talking about here.

There must be this atmosphere of unity before we can go to the next level of prayer. You can't be united in prayer as a group if everybody has been gossiping all the time. You can't all have the same purpose or be "with one accord" (Acts 4:24) when half the congregation hates the other half. Therefore, we must learn how to walk, talk, and think in love before we can ever be united. I really believe that unity in prayer is of the utmost importance to the Body of Christ at this hour. The prayer of unity will bring the power of God into manifestation to a group of believers every time. Jesus said, "For where two or three are gathered together in my name, there I am in the midst of them" (Matt. 18:20), but before in verse 19, He spoke on the power of two praying in agreement. Often we are quick to say, "Oh I am in agreement with you brother!" But how do you really know if someone is really in agreement with you? If we truly had this agreement that Jesus spoke of then we would have the results He spoke of as well. Jesus said "if two of you shall agree on earth" then it would be "done for them of my Father which is in heaven." This prayer of agreement requires much more than mere lip service. Pastor Thomas would always say, "If someone turns their plate with you then you know they are in agreement with you." With this criterion, you will find there are far fewer in agreement with you than you may have thought; the good news is that you only need one to get the job done.

Now, I am truly blessed to be a part of believers that know how to pray both in the natural and in the spirit as well (I Cor. 14:14-15). But sad to say, we "tongue-talking" believers rarely achieve this unity in prayer. Now, let me clarify this a little more. In praise and worship, which is the highest form of prayer, we unite more often than we do in intercessory prayer. Oh, dear friend reaching unity is a beautiful thing. It is a goal worth every effort or pain that it may take to achieve. When you get, as the Bible says "with one accord" or with one purpose or mind, you'll never forget it. Sometimes it seems like surfing. You catch that one ride of a life time and spend the rest of the summer trying to catch another one just like it. Just like with surfing, all the conditions have to be just right for that perfect wave to come to shore, but if you are in the wrong place or not prepared when the wave comes you will miss it.

> *To catch the waves of revival that is coming to the shore, we must first be prepared and then we must be in the right place.*

Dear friend, there is a wave coming to the shore, a wave of revival, but we must prepare ourselves. We must get into place and be ready! If you are called to be a preacher and you are trying to be a singer, stop singing and start preaching. If you are called to be a teacher, then start teaching to the glory of God. Not only do we need to get into position, we need to keep ourselves ready by continually feeding on the Word of God and preparing our hearts through prayer and fasting. They do go together you know. My friend, if Jesus had to fast for forty days to get Himself ready for public ministry, don't you think you and I will have to fast sometimes too? When I took a surfing class back during my college days, the coach had us doing push-ups and running three miles on the beach. I thought he was crazy. All I wanted to do was surf. When I got on that board and started paddling out in those waves, I knew why he made us exercise because my arms felt like Jello. My arms were so weak. Don't let this wave of revival catch you unprepared and in the wrong spot. Get into shape! Get into place, and keep your eyes peeled for a move of God like we have never seen before.

As I was saying, about unity in prayer, we must leave all bad attitudes at home as well as our personal opinions. Just stick with the Word of God. We must come together in prayer for God's purpose, and His purpose alone, to be fulfilled in this earth, if we are going to see this wave come to shore. The wave of revival will come before Jesus comes back to earth, but if we are going to see it, we must get busy and hasten His coming.

> *Seeing then that all these things shall be dissolved, what manner of persons ought ye to be in all holy conversation and godliness, Looking for and hasting unto the coming of the day of God, wherein the heavens being on fire shall be dissolved, and the elements shall melt with fervent heat? 2 Peter 3:11-12*

Notice verse 11 says, "hasting unto the coming". We have a part to play in the timing of events. Notice the gospel of the kingdom must be preached in all the world for a witness before Jesus comes back. Who is doing the preaching? The angels? No. Jesus? No. We are the preachers, God's witnesses on this earth. Romans 8:23 tells us that we who have received the Spirit "groan within ourselves." Groaning is a deep prayer given by the Spirit in the inward most parts of the belly. What are we groaning about? We are not groaning for Cadillac's, new houses or cars, but we as the Body of Christ should be groaning for the redemption of our bodies. This can only be received when Christ returns. In other words, we should have an eternal mindset and groan for His return.

> *Then came the word of the LORD by Haggai the prophet, saying, Is it time for you, O ye, to dwell in your ceiled houses, and this house lie waste? Now therefore thus saith the LORD of hosts; Consider your ways. Ye have*

sown much, and bring in little; ye eat, but ye have not enough; ye drink, but ye are not filled with drink; ye clothe you, but there is none warm; and he that earneth wages earneth wages to put it into a bag with holes. Thus saith the LORD of hosts; Consider your ways. Go up to the mountain, and bring wood, and build the house; and I will take pleasure in it, and I will be glorified, saith the LORD. Ye looked for much, and, lo, it came to little; and when ye brought it home, I did blow upon it. Why? saith the LORD of hosts. Because of mine house that is waste, and ye run every man unto his own house. Therefore the heaven over you is stayed from dew, and the earth is stayed from her fruit. And I called for a drought upon the land, and upon the mountains, and upon the corn, and upon the new wine, and upon the oil, and upon that which the ground bringeth forth, and upon men, and upon cattle, and upon all the labour of the hands. Haggai 1:3-11

Notice that the people in Haggai's day were like a lot of people today. We want God to do so much for us, but we don't want to do anything for Him. We use our faith to believe God for nice houses, new cars, new clothes and a host of other things, but are we building God's House? In New Testament passages, the Amplified Bible, for the word "believe," will add in parentheses "trusts in, clings to, relies on" in order to help us see more accurately what the word "believe" means in the Greek (for example see John 3:16). Recently, I began to notice so many saints saying, "I am believing God for this" or "I am believing God for that." I also noticed how hard it was to get many of them to honor their commitments to do God's work and help in the church. Once while preparing for a sermon, I heard the Lord say, "What can I believe (trust in, cling to, rely on) you for?" That showed me how often we use God and forget that we have a two-way covenant with God. Sure God will bless you with a new car, but don't start acting funny when God needs you to pick up some people across town for church. Don't give God a busy signal because you spend all of your time on that job that He blessed you with when the church calls for help! Avail yourself for God's work. Offer your gifts and talents to God and be a part of what God is doing in the earth today, building His House.

> **What can God believe you for?**

FASTING AND PRAYER

Remember, the key ingredients of the United Prayer are that they all were in one place, all were with one accord, and by the help of the Holy Spirit, all were with one voice. I also shared that, although this is our goal when uniting in prayer, there are many opposing forces that would try and prevent us from achieving it. I also briefly touched on a tool that is crucial in tearing down enemy strongholds that hinder the unity that God desires for His children to walk in, fasting. Extended periods of fasting are essential to our personal preparation for ministry as well as preparing us corporately. As we have seen in the first chapters of the book of Acts, unity is a must for the Body of Christ in order to bring about the waves of revival that God desires to pour out on this land. Fasting is such a powerful tool that it is no wonder why the devil works so hard to keep the Body of Christ confused and divided on the subject. To date, there are a number of good resources on the benefits of fasting, the various types of biblical fasts, and their applications. The purpose of this section is not to go into depth on the subject but to briefly stress the importance of fasting in preparing the Church for revival and achieving unity.

Fasting is something that I was not accustomed to growing up. It was not taught in the denominational church that I grew up in, nor did we practice it in my family. My first encounter with fasting was when a Pentecostal roommate in college described it to me as a "crowbar" that would give you some extra leverage with God. It apparently worked better for him than it did me, for by the second day of my attempted three-day fast, I had intense stomach pains and rushed to the fridge to make myself a turkey sandwich. I later learned that the proper motivation for fasting was to CHANGE ME, NOT GOD. Fasting is for the purpose of quieting our flesh (in some cases bringing it under) so that we can hear from God. I like to think of it as a spiritual alignment much like one that the front-end of a car needs after hitting too many potholes. Actually, that is all that is required in obtaining the blessings that God has already promised us, simply getting in line with Him.

It was not until I joined Agape Faith Center in Gainesville, FL that I got the courage to fast again. Some say that you don't have to wait for the church to call a fast; you can fast anytime the Spirit leads you to. While this is certainly true, if it had not been for my pastor calling our church to fast each Tuesday from 6AM till 6PM, I would have continued to exempt myself from fasting all together, ignoring the Spirit's leading. There were those in our church who spoke of three, seven, ten, and twenty-one-day fasts, but I had become the master of the six-to-six fast and was quiet content.

> **Fasting is a way to change us, not God.**

Life was good. I thought I was really spiritual. Then I met my fiancée, Martha. She was such an attractive, vibrant, friendly young lady, and so delightful to be around. Her love for Jesus was so obvious. She had such godly wisdom and counsel, and she was a great listener too! We had so many things in common and so much to share with each other. But there was this one minor detail; she was Black, and I was White. I knew the very mention of such a thing would cause a major uproar with my family back in Georgia. More importantly, it was apparent that God was putting us together. So, I finally got up enough courage to ask her to marry me. Thank God she said, "Yes," and at the appropriate time, we announced our engagement.

We first announced our plans to our parents. I was certain that Martha's mom, Evangelist Jackson, this prayerful, godly woman that I had heard so much about, would surely rejoice with us. It was just my parents that I was going to need much prayer and courage to face. The announcement to Evangelist Jackson did not go as I had planned. It was as if she was operating on a different plane than me. Her reply blazed right past the natural excitement that Martha and I had. She said something like, "I don't care if he is green with purple polka dots. I just want to make sure that it's God's will." I thought to myself, "Didn't she just hear us say we believed God was leading us together. Didn't she think that we had prayed about this already?" But, no! The next thing she said was even more unnerving. She called the family on a seven day fast. Not only did Martha do strange stuff like fast more than 12 hours, but she had two sisters that jumped on the bandwagon too! I knew that certainly God would understand and let me off the fast because I had to work. Talk about a hard sale; try and tell God that you are not going on a fast that was for the sole purpose of making sure that you were marrying the right one. As you probably guessed, I had to give up that non-sense and join the fast.

I survived till Saturday, and thought that this would be a great day to stay in bed all day. But it just so happened that the church had a work day, and Martha and I had to be there. As the day progressed, Pastor couldn't help but notice me walking at a snail's pace and about to fall out. He asked me what was wrong. I told him about the fast. I was hoping he would tell me to go home, but instead he gave me probably the greatest fasting secret that I have ever heard. He said, "Brother Kent, you have to switch gas tanks." He told me to sit down for a few minutes and mediate on scriptures about God's strength. He knew if I didn't tap into my spiritual gas tank quickly, it would be all over. My natural gas tank was on E-minus! Amazingly, I got strength to get up and finish the day.

> **When fasting, you must switch from your natural gas tank to your spiritual one.**

I thought surely, the last day would be a breeze since we would be at church praising God for most of the day. It did start out that way; until the middle of the worship service, I turned around and saw some unexpected guest, three of my family members from Georgia. Putting two plus two together, I figured something must be up since they drove four hours to join us unannounced, and plus, I knew they were none too happy about our marriage plans. After church, one of our unexpected guests, my daddy, insisted that we go out and get some lunch. I tried to tell him without making a big scene that although Martha and I would not be eating until later, we would just take some juice and join them. Maybe that was so obvious that even a man that didn't fast caught on to that real quick. My daddy said there in the Piccadilly Cafeteria line, "That perishing and praying won't change me!"

After we got that settled, we proceeded to the dining area. The dinner conversation was a bit frigid for a while, but things soon began to thaw. I mean really thaw! For some strange reason, the hot topic of the day, our engagement, was somehow side-stepped and turned to my time serving as the interim-pastor of my family's church back in Georgia. (My dad was not a part of this other agenda; he stuck to his original mission, the engagement.) I was being questioned and attacked for things I had taught. Apparently, things I had taught were all being "straightened out" by the new pastor that came after me. Martha nudged me under the table and said under her breath, "Aren't you going to say something?" Honestly, by day seven of the fast, my flesh was so under that they could have called me almost anything and I wouldn't have cared. I finally piped up and said a thing or two in my defense, but by the grace that I had tapped into on the fast, I was able to let it just roll off of me.

God shielding me from personal attacks through prayer and fasting was one thing, but the miracle of all miracles occurred four years after Martha and I were married. For the first time since our marriage, my parents came to spend the weekend with us. We had a glorious time together! This time around, I almost got in the flesh when my daddy bought my wife a bigger Christmas present than mine. Seriously though, he was making a big fuss over his new daughter-in-law. That "perishing and praying" did change my daddy, and we have a wonderful relationship today. He and mom have come to our rescue in tough financial times more than once when there was no one else to turn to.

In the words of my mother-in-law, "Prayer changes things!" Prayer and fasting is not something she just talks about, it is an integral part of her life. She will also tell you with the quickness, "Some kind only come out by prayer and fasting." Mom is definitely on to something here that the Church by and large is missing today. In Mark 9, the man came to the disciples with his son possessed by a dumb spirit. The disciples were unable to cast the devil out of the boy. When the man saw Jesus coming down from the mountain, he told Jesus how the disciples could not cast the devil out. After Jesus cast the devil out of the boy, the disciples asked Jesus in private why they couldn't cast the devil out. His answer was startling! He said, "This kind can come forth by nothing, but by prayer and fasting" (Mark 9:29). We know that earlier Jesus had been led into the wilderness to be tempted of the devil (Matt. 4:1, Mark 1:13). If He was led of the Spirit to be tempted, the fast certainly must have been Spirit-led as well. This extended time of prayer and fasting had obviously prepared Jesus with the power and anointing He needed to get the job done! There is a message here for the Church today: there are certain kinds of demons that will only come out "by PRAYER and FASTING." At first, I thought the passage meant that prayer and fasting was needed to cast out "dumb devils." Until later, I realized that "this kind" is the kind of devil that you have been rebuking, and despite all, he "just ain't 'buking!" There are just some devils that aren't going anywhere until we turn down our plates.

We in the Church today should be so humble and honest as the disciples were to ask, "Why we don't have the power we need to cast out devils?" Many would correct me here to say, "But we do have the power! Jesus already gave it to us!" Legally you are right, but in actuality, if we were honest, we would have to admit that most of us are certainly not seeing that kind of results. Jesus gave us the answer right here in the account of the boy with a dumb spirit. Invariably you will find yourself in an assignment or facing a battle and the power required to succeed will come forth only by PRAYER AND FASTING.

This leads me to a serious problem in some faith circles today. Many faith teachers have popularized a teaching that "long" fasts are no longer necessary. According to these teachers, all that is necessary is a "fasted lifestyle." I am not sure if you ask three people what a "fasted lifestyle" is, if you would get the same answer. Years ago when I first read about a "fasted lifestyle," it was explained as never eating all that you want, or keeping the flesh in check by never satisfying it. That is a worthy goal indeed, but I have found few that attempt, much less achieve, this goal. My point here is not to cause contention over the issue, for there are many that firmly believe this way today. But I must caution that we must always follow what Jesus taught and demonstrated in the Word over what man says. After all, Jesus said, "When ye fast" not "if you fast" (Matt. 6:16).

Flesh has a way of masquerading itself. Like dealing with an unruly child, you must take control of your flesh and discipline it! The rod of correction for a child is most often thought of as a belt or a paddle, although it really is whatever will get the attention of a wayward child and bring them back into submission.

> But I keep under my body, and bring it into subjection: lest that by any means, when I have preached to others, I myself should be a castaway. 1 Corinthians 9:27

This verse has got to be one of the most sobering warnings for preachers that I have ever read. You may be gifted and tremendously anointed when it comes to preaching to others, but if you don't keep your flesh "under" subjection, you will eventually find yourself washed up on the shore. If you find your flesh being unruly, there is one sure way to bring it "under," fasting. If for no other reason, I say "long" fasts are necessary to bring your flesh into submission. This doesn't happen the first day or even the second, but somewhere around the third day, the flesh will whimper and submit. Beware though, the flesh is not going to give up without a fight, but with God's grace and strength you can make it through your Spirit-led fast and bring your flesh "under."

There is much power made available to you when you trust God on a fast, and even more power made available when we fast together as a body of believers. Another way the devil keeps us divided as a church, besides gossip, is prayerlessness. I always thought that since a "house divided against itself ... cannot stand" (Mark 3:25), then surely division was the strongman. Then I learned about the sin of prayerlessness (1 Sam. 12:23). Given what we have learned so far, if gossip can separate the closest of friends, then certainly prayer can bring them together (Prov. 16:28)! Therefore prayerlessness is stronger than division, or in other words, it is the major cause of it. The only way to run division out of your church and keep it out is by praying together.

> *Prayerlessness is stronger than division.*
> *Only the house that prays together will*
> *stay together.*

The devil also stops us from receiving God's grace by tempting us to be lifted up in pride. God can only give us grace when we are humble, "humble enough to receive it" (James 4:6 AMP). Prayer and fasting is one of the best ways that we can humble ourselves. In so doing, we overcome the devil's tactics of prayerlessness and pride. It also helps us to root out those things that hinder our unity. The fast that God chooses always loosens "the bands of wickedness," undoes "the heavy burdens," lets "the oppressed go free," and "breaks every yoke" (Isa. 58:6). Fasting helps us to get to the point where we are humble enough to confess our faults one to another. When we confess our faults to each other instead of gossiping and backbiting, then we truly can "pray one for another, that ye may be healed." Our prayers then become "heartfelt" and "effective" making "tremendous power available dynamic in its working" (James 5:16 AMP).

CHAPTER 6

SPIRITUAL WARFARE

It is high time we in the Body of Christ wake up and take back what the devil has stolen from us. We must unite together in prayer as never before. From what I know about revival history, intense prayer and consecration has always preceded it. It seems as if modern day Charismatics know all the right things to say and all the right scriptures to quote, but when it comes down to prayer and fasting many seem to come up short. We are living in a McDonald's generation where everything is quick and easy. My friend, if you are going to be successful in prayer, you must develop perseverance. You must lock in with "bulldog grip tenacity" and never give up. There are no quick fixes in prayer. You can't just push a few buttons and flip a few switches and obtain revival. Nobody wants to sacrifice anymore, and if it calls for suffering, you can count most modern day Christians out. I always like to talk with the old-timers who have been through some things in their life, who have endured hard times. I've met people who may not know all the "right" modern day faith confessions, but they know how to pray and get in contact with God. They know how to turn their plates and shut themselves in. That's right! They shut themselves in until they get results and hear from heaven. This is the kind of prayer warriors that we need in order to bring about revival.

GROANING IN THE SPIRIT

I thank God for my pastor, Ron Thomas, who taught quiet extensively on the subject of groaning in the spirit. Although, I had been praying in other tongues for years when I met him, I never knew about groaning in the spirit. Pastor once taught on the subject and shared how the Lord told him that if this message wasn't taught that it would be lost from this generation. Judging from the lack of teaching on the subject, I would have to agree that Pastor Thomas' assessment was correct.

Once we concluded a prayer seminar with a session on groaning in the spirit. When Pastor Thomas finished teaching, we all got on our knees and groaned in the spirit for more than 15 minutes. The power of God came in the room so strong that the Holy Ghost began to fill people with the Spirit without anyone even laying hands on them. The next morning at our Sunday service we continued in the spirit of prayer by getting on our faces before God. Throughout the entire service, pastor would teach for a few minutes on prayer and then have us groan in the spirit for 15 minute at a time. As we continued to pray this way, I heard in the spirit a jealous demon say, "I can't stay here if you keep praying like that." That's when you know you've got the devil on the run. Prayer and the Word are our most effective weapons. These are the kind of experiences that are not available to just the casual observers. God rewards those who diligently seek Him.

> *Prayer and the Word are our most effective weapons.*

Groaning in the spirit is easier to recognize than it is to describe. This type of prayer, as the name suggests, is a deep groaning that comes from the belly. When you hear it, it usually brings to mind giving birth and is sometime referred to as travail or travailing in prayer. At times, the travail is so intense that you may see the person bending over, holding their belly. When a person really gets over into travail, it is not so easy for them to come out of this prayer. They will usually remain in this prayer mode for a while.

> *Likewise the Spirit also helpeth our infirmities: for we know not what we should pray for as we ought: but the Spirit itself maketh intercession for us with groanings which cannot be uttered. Romans 8:26*

Paul describes groaning in the spirit in Romans 8:26 when he says, "The Spirit maketh intercession for us with groanings which cannot be uttered." Some make no distinction here between praying in the spirit and groaning in the spirit. I have heard others even off-load the entire burden of prayer onto the Holy Spirit as if they have no part at all in the prayer. They describe the Spirit praying before God's face in heaven on their behalf apart from them because of the phrase "the Spirit maketh intercession for us," but that seems strange since the Holy Spirit now lives inside the believer, in our bellies (John 7:38). This verse makes much more sense in conjunction with Acts 2:4 where we first learn about being filled with the Spirit. This verse explains that as the believers "were all filled with the Holy Ghost," they "began to speak with other tongues, as the Spirit gave them utterance." When the believer fully yields to the Spirit and removes themselves from the equation, this God-given utterance flows freely. In intercession, when the believer so yields they will find this place where the Spirit is doing the praying and not them.

Of course, the intercession is still coming through the yielded vessel, but it becomes obvious that the source is the Spirit of God.

The Amplified Bible renders the phrase "groanings which cannot be uttered" as, "unspeakable yearnings *and* groanings too deep for utterance." You cannot groan deeply in a nonchalant manner. Deep groaning will deeply involve or even absorb you at times, yet it doesn't come out in words or articulate speech; it comes out in deep groans. I have found that this prayer kicks in often when I am going through an intense trial and have run out of words. Many times in prayer, I will sense the Spirit leading me just to be quiet. At this point with my eyes closed, I focus only on Jesus and His glory. Actually, this sounds easier than it really is. Maybe it's just me, but I tend to be a motor-mouth in prayer or either find my mind racing a hundred miles an hour about the things I am facing. Once I am able to reach this quiet place, in His presence, many times the Spirit will have me just stay there. After a while, sometimes a long while, deep groanings will start inside of my belly. Many times I have dropped to my knees, ready to quit in ministry. After meeting with God this way, I would get up with my joy restored and ready to continue doing what God assigned me to do. Normal praying in the spirit sounds like sentences in an unknown language, but groaning in the spirit is just that, moans and groans. As perplexing to the mind as this may sound, this prayer always gets the job done and lifts the heavy burden.

I personally think Hannah was in this mode when she went to the temple of the Lord in Shiloh. She made a vow to God out of her affliction that if God would open her womb and grant her a son, she would dedicate him back to God "all the days of his life" (1 Sam. 1:11). Unlike some, Hannah paid promptly on her vow and gave Samuel back to God. While she was in the temple praying, Eli noticed that her lips were moving, but he couldn't hear her voice. The reason I think she may have been groaning: number one, she was in much affliction over her childless condition and number two, Eli thought she was drunk. I am sure others before Hannah had come to the temple and prayed a silent prayer to God. Surely Eli was not perplexed about the silence. Even though nothing was audible, something was happening on the inside of Hannah. The Bible says she "spake in her heart; only her lips moved, but her voice was not heard" (1 Sam. 1:13). She told the priest, "No my lord, I am a woman of a sorrowful spirit; I have drunk neither wine nor strong drink, but have poured my soul before the Lord" (1 Sam. 1:15). After that Eli told her to go home for God had granted her petition!

Jesus also prayed this way before Lazarus was raised. The first time this was mentioned, the Bible says that not only did Jesus weep (John 11:35) when Mary ran to meet him being grief-stricken about the death of her brother Lazarus, but he "groaned in the spirit, and he was troubled" also (John 11:33). He then asked where they had laid Lazarus. At Lazarus' tomb, the Bible says, that Jesus "again groaning in himself" (John 11:38). After this prayer, he commands them to take the stone away! Martha, obviously missing the moment, injects, "Lord, by this time he stinketh" being dead four days. Jesus with extreme focus, not allowing the emotions and the unbelief of the mourners to pull him off course, reminds them that he had said, "if thou wouldest believe, thou shouldest see the glory of God" (John 11:40). Next, his prayer-connection with the Father was truly astounding, for he simply looks up and says, "Father, I thank thee that thou hast heard me; And I knew that thou hearest me always." Apparently the entire prayer was given for the bystander's benefit, for he said, "I said it, that they may believe that thou hast sent me" (John 11:41-42). Despite the unbelief of so many onlookers, Lazarus came forth at Jesus' command, and everyone present that day did see the glory of God.

The "groaning which cannot be uttered" in Romans 8:26 taken in its context, is linked with the "glory which shall be revealed in us" in the preceding verses, Romans 8:18-25. Paul continues to explain why the Father would subject the creation to such suffering. He did it in hope, the hope or expectation of the sons of God being manifested (Rom. 8:19) and the creation being freed from corruption of this present world into the liberty of the sons of God (Rom. 8:21). Because of this corruption, the whole creation groans and travails together in pain (Rom. 8:22). The mountains, the hills, and the trees know that the earth is cursed, and are "groaning in pain" at this present time. But one day soon the mountains and the hills shall break forth into singing and the trees will even clap their hands when the curse is removed for planet earth (Isa. 55:12). Soon, some in the animal kingdom will drop their guards while others will drop their killer instincts as the wolf and the lamb lie down together and the lion eats straw like an ox (Isa. 11:6-7, 65:25). The question is, why

> **When we yield to the Spirit in groanings,
> the results are always glorious.**

isn't the pinnacle of God's creation, man who is made in His own image, getting on board with the groaning? Paul says that we who have the firstfruits of the Spirit "groan within ourselves" as we await "the redemption of our bodies" (Rom. 8:23). I like to think of it this way that we are groaning for glory. Things may well be difficult at the present and you may be in much pain, but the Word says we who have the Spirit should be groaning. When we do so, the results will be glorious.

*Before she travailed, she brought forth; before her pain
came, she was delivered of a man child. Who hath heard
such a thing? who hath seen such things? Shall the earth*

be made to bring forth in one day? or shall a nation be born at once? for as soon as Zion travailed, she brought forth her children. Shall I bring to the birth, and not cause to bring forth? saith the LORD: shall I cause to bring forth, and shut the womb? saith thy God.
Isaiah 66:7-9

Isaiah asks the unthinkable, "Shall the earth be made to bring forth in a day? Or shall a nation be born at once?" In 1948, that's exactly what happened. After nearly 2000 years of being scattered abroad without a home, the U.N. officially recognized Israel as a nation and millions of Jews were allowed to return to their homeland. The prophet not only gives an astounding prediction here, but he gives a key prayer principle as well: "as soon as Zion travailed, she brought forth her children." In the Scripture, Zion was first seen as a hill captured by King David and his brave men. Later, the word grew to include the city of Jerusalem, the entire nation of Israel, and eventually grew to encompass all the people of God.

We have already seen that we, as "lively stones" are "built up a spiritual house" for God to dwell in (1 Pet. 2:5). God said He would lay in Zion a chief Cornerstone upon which the whole building or the Church would be built upon. Praise God, Jesus, our Lord, is that Cornerstone. Peter goes on to say that we who were "not a people" are now "the people of God" (1 Pet. 2:10). We as the people of God and members of the Body of Christ are now included in Zion. Now, what happens when the people of God, the Church, begins to travail in prayer? You guessed it, sons will be born!

> **As soon as the Church travails, she brings forth sons.**

58

After the fall of man in the garden, God prophesied that deliverance would come through the seed of the woman and that this seed would bruise the head of the serpent (Gen. 3:15). Paul, referring back to the fall, points out that it was the woman who was first deceived by the serpent. "Notwithstanding," he says, "she shall be saved in childbearing" if she continues in faith, love, holiness with sobriety (1 Tim. 2:15). No doubt Paul is showing the powerful role of the godly mother who through childbearing and childrearing furthers the gospel by training a child to fear and serve God. But what about the Church, the Bride of Christ, as we assume our childbearing role? In Romans 7, Paul states that the believer is dead to the Law through the body of Christ. Now being dead to the Law, we "should be married to another, even to him who is raised from the dead that we should bring forth fruit unto God" (Rom. 7:4). If any church is going to survive, it must evangelize and birth new born babies into the kingdom of God, but as we have seen demonstrated in this section, groaning in the spirit or travailing prayer is necessary for bringing these sons forth.

WARRING IN TONGUES

For some strange reason warring in tongues is a very controversial subject in the Body of Christ. If our Lord and King is referred to as the Captain of the Host (Josh. 5:14), and we are commanded to put on the whole armor of God for prayer (Eph. 6:10-17), then why would it surprise someone that our prayers would come out with a battle cry? Even when I was in a denominational church we used to sing, "Onward Christian soldiers marching as to war." Soldiers sing war songs as they are marching to battle, not nursery rhymes.

I have heard a minister conclude that because warring in tongues was directed at Satan rather than "unto God" as I Corinthians 14:2 prescribes, it was therefore not of God. I have had people question me because I rebuked Satan while I was praying to God. As I get over into prayer about a situation, the Holy Ghost will rise up in me with boldness to rebuke the devil if he is involved. You might say that we are supposed to be talking to God. Yes, but the Word also tells us to give the devil no place (Eph. 4:27). Jesus also tells us that the believing ones will cast out devils in His name (Mark 16:17), so I just deal with the devil while I'm talking with my Daddy. Paul puts it this way, "The weapons of our warfare are not carnal, but are mighty THROUGH GOD to the pulling down of strongholds" (II Cor. 10:4). This teaches us that true warfare is always THROUGH GOD and never separated from Him.

> *Our warfare is always mighty through God and never separated from Him.*

Prayer, when coupled with the Word of God, becomes our most vital weapon. Paul admonishes us to "put on the whole armour of God" so that we "may be able to STAND against the wiles of the devil" (Eph. 6:11). Notice the last piece of the armor, the sword of the Spirit, that we are to take on in the fight against the demonic hosts in the heavenly places: "take … the sword of the Spirit, which is the word of God: Praying always with all prayer and supplications in the Spirit" (Eph. 6:17). Our prayers have to be loaded with the Word of God, yet inspired by the Spirit of God. If you try to deal with the devil on your own, you will get squashed every time. The Spirit of God is sent to help us. We must never enter into warfare without him guiding us. The Bible tells us clearly that it is the anointing of the Holy Spirit that destroys the yokes of bondage (Isa. 10:27). The Spirit of God or the Anointing was upon Jesus to "preach deliverance to the captives, and recovering of sight to the blind, to set at liberty them that are bruised" (Luke 4:18). How much more do you think we will need the Holy Ghost when we face the enemy? We are always quick to quote, "Resist the devil and he will flee from you." But let's look at the whole verse.

> *Submit yourselves therefore to God. Resist the devil, and*
> *he will flee from you. James 4:7*

You had better be submitted to God before you go up against the devil. The point being that if you and God are co-laborers and work in covenant together, why would it surprise you if your tongues to God would come out with a warring sound when you are up against the devil? We must rely on the help of the Holy Ghost. Remember, praying in the spirit is a powerful way to yield to the Holy Spirit and keep your mind out of the picture. This allows the Spirit of God to pray through us freely and to wreak havoc on the devils kingdom.

    The first time I can remember warring in tongues or rebuking the devil in tongues was when I was blessing someone's house. I went through the house commanding the devils to leave and anointing the rooms with oil. If you are keen to the Spirit, you can tell if a house is blessed or not, simply by the atmosphere in the house. Peace has a way of meeting you at the door when you enter; on the other hand, strife and division will also greet you. After blessing the house in Jesus' Name, I also like to take a bottle of anointing oil and go through every room in the house and anoint them.

    This particular night, I was drawn to a statute or an idol that looked as if it was from the Far East. It actually reminded me of a Buddha statute. I laid my hand upon the figure and without even thinking the Holy Spirit inside me recoiled. The hair on the back off my neck stood at attention, and all of a sudden this tongue came out of my belly that sounded like a machine gun going off. Shortly after the prayer ended, I knew that the power of the devil was broken over that figure. The owners of that house should have prayed about it before purchasing the statute. The Holy Spirit would have certainly warned them if they were tuned in to His channel, but some people let their desire for nice things get them into trouble. Has that ever happened to you? We have to really be careful because many people, especially foreign countries where witchcraft is prevalent, put curses on statutes, dolls, trinkets, etc.

God told Joshua and company not to bring any accursed thing into the camp for it would contaminate the whole camp. Did they listen? No. Somebody SAW something they thought they couldn't do without and they snuck it home (Josh. 7:1). This cursed thing caused the whole nation to be defeated in battle. Furthermore, the sin of this one man caused his whole household to die a horrible death; they were stoned and burned. We must not be fooled. Our sins not only affect us, but they will affect our families as well. The Bible says our sins will be remembered as far as four generations (Num. 14:18). You may ask what is cursed and what is blessed? That's a good question. Let's examine this account a little further.

> *And ye, in any wise keep yourselves from the accursed thing, lest ye make yourselves accursed, when ye take of the accursed thing, and make the camp of Israel a curse, and trouble it. But all the silver, and gold, and vessels of brass and iron, are consecrated unto the LORD: they shall come into the treasury of the LORD.* Joshua 6:18-19

God gave specific instructions on what to get and what to do with it after they got it. A'chan did not follow God's instructions.

As A'chan made his confession before all of Israel, he revealed that he SAW this "goodly Babylonish garment" among the spoils. God didn't even tell him to get that. A'chan also decided that he wanted to keep some consecrated things, silver and gold. He said he coveted them and hid them in his tent (Josh. 7:21). That is the same way the devil deceived Eve, and that is the same way he will deceive you if you'll let him. We are tempted and drawn away into sin by our own lust (James 1:14). The Bible says that the lust of the eyes, the lust of the flesh, and the pride of life are not of God, but of the world (I John 2:16). That's the reason we are told to be led of the Spirit of God. He will let you know on the inside what and what not to buy. If we listen to Him, we can avoid the trouble A'chan got into.

Now, getting back to the subject of warring in the spirit, let's look at a helpful verse.

> *To another the working of miracles, to another prophecy, to another the ability to distinguish between spirits, to another various kinds of tongues, to another the interpretation of tongues. 1 Corinthians 12:10 RSV*

> *To another the working of miracles; to another prophecy; to another discerning of spirits; to another divers kinds of tongues; to another the interpretation of tongues: 1 Corinthians 12:10*

The Revised Standard Version here uses "various kinds of tongues" whereas the King James Version uses "divers kinds of tongues." That obviously means that there is more than one kind of tongues. That lets me know that if you spoke in the same kind of tongue all the time, you are not operating in various kinds of tongues. Paul makes mention of "diversities of tongues" again at the end of the chapter, but this time he places it in a list with other ministries:

> *Now ye are the body of Christ, and members in particular. And God hath set some in the church, first apostles, secondarily prophets, thirdly teachers, after that miracles, then gifts of healings, helps, governments, diversities of tongues. Are all apostles? are all prophets? are all teachers? are all workers of miracles? Have all the gifts of healing? do all speak with tongues? do all interpret?* 1 Corinthians 12:27-30

The Revised Standard Version uses the same phrase, "various kinds of tongues," in both places. It is obvious in verse 28 that he is referring to a ministry of tongues. In verse 30, he asks the question, "Do all speak with tongues?" Well, the obvious answer is no, but that doesn't mean that all can't pray in the spirit. In Acts 2:4, we see that all 120 of them were filled with the Holy Ghost and began to speak with other tongues as the Spirit gave them utterance. We could say it like this and still be true, they were all filled with the Holy Ghost and (they all) began to speak with other tongues. I Corinthians 14:5 says, "I would that ye all spoke with other tongues." Notice I Corinthians 14:18-19, "I thank my God, I speak in tongues more than ye all: Yet in the church I had rather speak five words with my understanding." We see that Paul therefore did most of his speaking in tongues somewhere other than in the church. Since the operation of "divers kinds of tongues" requires an interpreter for the edification of the whole church, we can conclude that the majority of Paul's speaking in tongues was probably in prayer as he explains in 1 Corinthians 14:14-15.

There is a ministry for the body or church called diversities or various kinds of tongues. This ministry is not given to all, although all believers can speak with tongues (Mark 16:17). Many ministers explain this ministry as just one that gets up gives a message in tongues and interprets it to the church. But my question is where does the "various kinds of tongues" come in? Brother Derrick Prince in his sermon entitled *Diversities of Tongues* lists several kinds of tongues that the Lord has revealed to him such as praise, intercession, rebuke, and exhortation. I have noticed in my own prayer life that there is a tongue that usually comes forth when I am praying with others in group. This tongue has tremendous power, and I always know that it is demolishing the devil's stronghold in the given situation. It always reminds me of a machine gun. When the tongue stops, I always know that the job is done.

Many times the Lord has given me a burden to pray about something, and I tried to pray it through by myself to no avail. Victory was only achieved when I joined together with one or more believers who knew how to pray. Most of the times these war-like tongues would manifest in those prayer meetings, every time this gift manifested, we always got the victory. Some question why there was no interpretation to this type of tongue. It depends on what the purpose of the prayer is for. When a message in tongues is given before the church, it must always be followed with an interpretation so that all may be edified. Paul warns that there may be unbelievers present that certainly would think you were all nuts! On the other hand, when this kind of warring-tongue comes forth against enemy strongholds with a group of believers, the group understands what is happening and an interpretation is not necessary. Although, the Holy Spirit will usually let someone in the prayer group know by way of a vision or an inward witness of some kind that the enemy's stronghold has been broken. It is so important that we come together as believers and let the Holy Ghost manifest like He wants to. Don't try to put the Holy Ghost in a box.

When various kinds of tongues manifest it usually produces one or more of the following: prophecy, the word of wisdom, word of knowledge, visions, interpretations, a release in praise and worship or some other outpouring of the Spirit. People will always be blessed because with various kinds of tongues you will have the right tongue to get the job done. Various kinds of tongues will shake the devil loose from the service and allow the Holy Ghost to have His way. Once, when this gift manifested in our intercessory prayer group, I saw a vision of a battle-torn army waving their white flags in surrender. I knew the devil was throwing in the towel because his stronghold had been broken. This is why the proper understanding and proper use of our weapons are so important. Someone's salvation, healing, deliverance, or even their very life, could depend on it.

STRATEGY FOR YOUR CITY

In the last section, we looked at Joshua and his encounter with the Captain of the Host (Josh. 5:14). Joshua approached this stranger and asked, "Art thou for us, or for our adversaries?" He replied, "Nay; but as captain of the host of the Lord am I now come" (Josh. 5:13-14). Remember, in planning to take your city for Jesus, always coordinate it with Him first. Don't try to get Jesus to endorse your plan. When you go to Jesus throw out your plan, and let Him give you His agenda. After all, He is the Captain of the Host; He already has the battle planned out for us. As Commander and Chief of God's army, we simply need to get on His side and follow His plan to a tee. If He tells you to march around your city walls for seven days and on the seventh time of the seventh day to let out a big shout of praise, then don't dare open your mouth on the sixth day and blow the whole thing. Do exactly what he says and win!

Fight the good fight of faith (I Tim. 6:12) by doing and saying exactly what Jesus says. Keep all of your opinions and feelings to yourself and speak the Word in faith. Leave all your show business at home. Don't try to be the Lone Ranger either and steal the show. There is no time for that kind of foolishness in this battle. If Jesus says to shout and sing, then shout and sing till He tells you to stop. If Jesus tells you to dance in the street, then dance and shout your little heart out right there in the street. If He tells your group to come against the spirit of Jezebel, then do it. Don't go around making up a bunch of demon names that you know nothing about. Do exactly what He says and nothing more.

> *Don't waste your time with spiritual warfare if you don't have a church home; you are already in rebellion.*

And last but not least, always work together with a body of believers. Don't try to shake the devil's kingdom if you don't even have a church home; you're already in rebellion. You are even subject to the spirit of witchcraft in this condition (I Sam. 15:23). Now if you just moved and are in between churches you are not in rebellion, but you must not delay this important decision. You must prayerfully and diligently seek out your new church home. Otherwise, while you are uncovered, the enemy will seize the opportunity to attack.

I remember being in between churches, in transition with no covering over my head. I thought I was really tearing down demonic strongholds with a few others in the same boat as I was. We were already in rebellion, not submitting to any pastor, forsaking the assembling of ourselves together with other believers (Heb. 10:25), and trying to resist the devil. We were trying to pull down enemy strongholds over territories. I am not talking about just personal attacks. We really thought we were taking on spirits over certain areas or establishments where the devil's activity was obvious. The devil was just laughing at us. He was "pulling the wool over our eyes" with his deception. Oh, I thank God that the Holy Ghost got through to me and let me know that I needed a covering. It is a cold and lonely feeling out there with no covering over your head. You feel that there is no place to call home and nobody to pray for you when you're in trouble. That is living in the danger zone. I got busy and found a church home where the Word of God was being taught. The devil had beat up on me for so long until I was humbled. I didn't care if my pastor told me to clean the toilet, I was so glad to be in a Bible believing church that knew how to pray. It was good to come out of the cold and to fellowship with people of like-faith. Paul dealt with this foolishness in Colossians.

Let no man beguile you of your reward in a voluntary humility and worshipping of angels, intruding into those things which he hath not seen, vainly puffed up by his fleshly mind, And not holding the Head, from which all the body by joints and bands having nourishment ministered, and knit together, increaseth with the increase of God. Colossians 2:18-19

Jesus let me know from this passage that I either needed to be a pastor or have a pastor over me. He didn't call me to be floating around there like the Lone Ranger disconnected from the body without a pastor. Hebrews 13:17 says, "Obey them that have the rule over you." You need not think that you are going to float around in the Body of Christ and nobody tells you what to do. Somebody is going to have the rule over you. Jesus has given you to some under shepherd somewhere. It is your job to go out and find him or her and get plugged into that flock. When I say get plugged in I mean get busy! You can't go around doing warfare with your head in the clouds. Always work with your local church. After all Jesus does, why wouldn't you?

> ***You either need to be a pastor or have one.***

Probably one of the most memorable prayer experiences that I ever had was when three of us brothers met to "bust the devil up." We had gotten all excited about prayer and wanted to tear the strongholds down over the city of Gainesville. We came together and began our time with praise and worship and then we got right down to business, pulling down strongholds. We started out like a bull in a china shop. A few minutes into this all-out war on the devil, I felt a little uneasy in my spirit, but I just ignored the Spirit's warning thinking I was so spiritual. I wasn't going to let anything get me off course (not even the Holy Ghost). Then totally unexpected, the Spirit of the Lord fell on me, and I began to dance in the spirit. I danced so hard until I fell out on the floor. Minutes afterwards, I began to prophesy. After our little prayer meeting adjourned, I took some time to write down the prophecy as much as I could. The message went like this:

> *Get over into the Spirit. Whatever it takes to get over in the Spirit, do it. You may say what does it take? For some it may take fasting from sex, for some TV, for some people, for some food, but whatever it takes to get your flesh quiet do it.*

> *You need to hear from Me. How many of you know what principalities are ruling over this city? How many of you know what the devil's strategy is in Gainesville? Did not I*

say in My Word that we are not unaware of Satan's schemes? You need to ask Me saith God and I will show you.

No army just goes to battle with just a brute show of might, scatter blasting. Battles are won through wise counsel and planning. You don't just up and go fight because you feel like fighting. You must coordinate it. Get a strategy, a plan of attack before you leave the barracks. Ask Me.

Remember the Persian Gulf War was fought with precision accuracy. Patriot and Tomahawk missiles were used. Missiles were launched with such precision that they went down chimneys. No one just blew up at random, but missiles were launched at well thought out targets.

Ask of Me and I will show you where your enemy is sleeping and give you missiles to go down his chimney into his bedroom and blow him up.

Use the weapons of your warfare. They are not carnal but spiritual. Rely on Me to give you the word of knowledge, word of wisdom, and discerning of spirits to name and locate your enemy.

The Lord also encouraged us for our zeal. He said He was looking for a people willing to learn of Him, to be taught in spiritual warfare. He also said that unity was so important in battle. We need to check with the General and find out what the Spirit's strategy is in this city. Not a blast here and there, but a unified effort to defeat the enemy. The Lord also told us that we didn't know what we were messing with. He told us that this was nothing to play with, but we needed to fight by His instruction.

After that message, we all repented and began to seek God's face for wisdom, for we realized that we had zeal, "but not according to knowledge" (Rom. 10:2). Let me just add that although Satan is a defeated foe and put under our feet (Eph. 1:22), he is not to be taken lightly, especially when dealing with principalities, powers, and rulers of the darkness that have been ruling in a city for years, maybe even centuries. Satan is brought to naught through Jesus Christ, but when we get in the flesh and try to be lone rangers, he can knock us for a loop. Satan is united, organized, and has a strategy for your city. Don't be fooled and try to tackle his works by yourself. Join up with the well-seasoned prayer warriors in your church that are submitted to the pastor and know how to follow the Spirit of God in prayer. This way, the prayer group is submitted to God's authority on this earth and has the proper covering.

Because of what Jesus accomplished on the cross, some choose to focus only on the fact that Satan was already defeated and therefore has no power. While that is true, people fail to see that the devil still receives power from those who blindly give it to him.

> *And the devil said unto him, All this power will I give thee, and the glory of them: for that is delivered unto me; and to whomsoever I will I give it. Luke 4:6*

He is no dummy. We have just fallen for his tricks and given him place by our disobedience. As mentioned earlier, people give Satan power when they yield their tongues to him. Just like you wouldn't have taken the Boy Scouts and tried to round up Al Capon and his mob, you wouldn't just waltz in and take over a well-established stronghold of the devil either. As a matter of fact, where do you think that Al Capon learned his tactics from anyway? Well of course, the god of this world, the devil himself (II Cor. 4:4). The point is it takes believers who know their authority and walk in the power of Jesus to take back what the devil has stolen from them.

Once, when the intercessors of our church met for the first time to pray for our morning service at our new location, I heard in the spirit a bunch of demons scream, "Oh no! Not that bunch. They know how to use the name of Jesus!" Demons tremble at the Name of Jesus. They can't stand for you to use the Name. When believers get together and do warfare against the devil in the Name of Jesus, he and his imps get real nervous. He will do anything he can to bust up your prayer meeting. He is not concerned about you selling chicken dinners or having dinner on the ground. When you start tearing his kingdom down with prayer, he will attack you with sickness, send car problems your way, or do just about anything to keep you from getting to church on Sunday morning. He is famous for stirring up strife in your household right before service so that you will be so churned up you won't be able to get into the spirit when you do make it to church. Those diversion tactics are just a few of the many that he will use to STOP YOUR PRAYER MEETING. You must walk in love to stay in the spirit because the devil knows that if you are not in the spirit then you can't do spiritual warfare.

In the earlier chapters, we have proved how important your love walk is in order to live a victorious life. Once when I was meditating on love scriptures, the devil that had been oppressing my mind slipped up and said, "I CAN'T STAY WHERE LOVE IS!" Love never fails (I Cor. 13:8), and if you never fail to walk in love, you will always be successful. That doesn't mean you will never slip up, but when you do, be quick to repent and start again. If you come to do spiritual warfare when you are in strife, the devil will laugh at you. To be effective at spiritual warfare, we must first submit to Jesus. Since Jesus is in heaven and you and I are still down here, that means that you and I need to submit to the men and women on this earth that Jesus has sent as pastors and other leaders in the Church. This is the Bible way. We must always do things according to the Word of God. Then and only then, can you resist the devil and expect him to flee from you. We must always remember that Jesus' number one agenda at the present is building His Church. While Jesus was on the earth he said, "I will build my church; and the gates of hell shall not prevail against it" (Matt. 16:18). It is important that we do spiritual warfare and take our cities back for God, but we must join the Captain of the Host's building project and not go around promoting our own.

> *The devil can't stay where love is.*

CHAPTER 7

ANSWERING THE CALL TO PRAYER

*Praying always with all prayer and supplication in the
Spirit, and watching thereunto with all perseverance and
supplication for all saints; And for me, that utterance may
be given unto me, that I may open my mouth boldly, to
make known the mystery of the gospel, For which I am an
ambassador in bonds: that therein I may speak boldly, as
I ought to speak.   Ephesians 6:18-20*

*I exhort therefore, that, first of all, supplications, prayers,
intercessions, and giving of thanks, be made for all men;
For kings, and for all that are in authority; that we may
lead a quiet and peaceable life in all godliness and honesty.
For this is good and acceptable in the sight of God our
Saviour; Who will have all men to be saved, and to come
unto the knowledge of the truth.   1 Timothy 2:1-4*

Pray without ceasing.   1 Thessalonians 5:17

Who is called to intercede? Is it just for a special group
of prayer warriors at your church? NO! Again, we
look at our familiar verses above to see just how all

of us are commanded to put on the whole armor of God. We all are also commanded to pray with all prayers and supplications in the Spirit for all saints. Remember intercessory prayer is not only praying for you and yours, it is praying for others. In our next verse, I Timothy, we are all exhorted that supplications, prayers, intercessions, and giving of thanks, be made for all men. The Bible doesn't leave any one out; we are all called to pray and pray without ceasing.

Although we should all answer the call to prayer, there are those who will be uniquely called to function in this body ministry just like some are anointed to the usher ministry or the music ministry. If you look at the list of offices in Ephesians 4:11, you will not find intercessor in that list of the five-fold ministry gifts. If you look in the list of motivations in Romans 12:6-9, you will not find intercessor either. If you look in the list of ministries in I Corinthians 12:28, you will not find the call of an intercessor specified there either, although, it would fall under the ministry of helps in that list.

> *Intercessors are the backbone of the ministry. Without them, the ministry could not go on.*

I remember specifically being called to be an intercessor. This call of an intercessor is not a glamorous one to say the least. Usually intercessors are in the background somewhere praying, going unnoticed and many times unrewarded in this life. I've heard my pastor say many times to the faithful few intercessors, "You are the backbone of the ministry. Without you the ministry could not go on." He also encouraged us many times by saying, "You will never know just how much your prayers are accomplishing until you get to heaven." Without that type of mind set you will get very discouraged as an intercessor. All helps ministries are important to the success of five-fold ministry to go out and win the battles just as Aaron and Hur were so vital to holding up Moses' arms in battle.

From our study on intercession, Abraham rose to the occasion with boldness to stand in the gap for Sodom and Gomorrah where his nephew, Lot, and his family resided. Nehemiah also did not just grieve about the news of his homeland's condition; he answered the call and was moved to pray for his nation. Now, the question at hand is what will you do? Will you answer the call to intercede? Intercession is one of the most selfless things that you can do; by definition, it is praying for someone other than yourself. What better way to apply the bond of perfectness to our brothers and sisters and strengthen God's House as we discussed earlier in Colossians 3:14? Let's remove ourselves from the selfishness of the "give me, give me" prayers and answer the call to pray for all saints, everywhere as stated in Ephesians 6:18-19.

There is a greater and more urgent call today than just praying for your neighbors and loved ones. I hope that from reading *Building God's House*, you see what the purpose of the building is all about. From one aspect we saw that we as lively stones are being built up for a spiritual habitation, a place for God to come and dwell, but the other purpose of our walls of this building is to KEEP the DEVIL OUT. Again in Nehemiah, the real reason for the disgrace and reproach was that Jerusalem's defenses were down and the devil saw them as NO THREAT. Once again recall the New Living Translation of Ezekiel 22:30, "Who would build again the wall of righteousness that GUARDS the land."

From this verse, it is easy to explain the events of 9-11. Oh, we all are so quick to take odds with the terrorist, but that is not where the real problem is. The problem is with the wall of righteousness that guards the land. You don't have to be a theologian to see that our walls had some serious holes in them.

My friend, God looks more so to the Church of America as the problem than the threat of terrorism. We have the weapons and the material to build a wall that will protect our land. You may well remember the words of 2 Chronicles 7:14 where God tells us that "If my people, who are called by my name, shall HUMBLE THEMSELVES, and PRAY, And SEEK MY FACE, And TURN FROM THEIR WICKED WAYS; then will I HEAR FROM HEAVEN, and will FORGIVE THEIR SINS, and will HEAL THEIR LAND." My friend God has told us what to do to save this land. The question is what are we doing with the awesome privilege that we have been given by God to intercede on behalf of the whole nation?

> *If the Church would pray with the unity of the Muslims, we could stop the waves of judgment that are heading towards this nation.*

Once again, recall that the time to pray for the nation is before judgment falls. Once judgment falls, it is too late. Shortly after 9-11 at a prayer and repentance service, the Lord gave me a vision of a multitude of Muslims praying together all facing the same way and with their faces to the ground. At that time this was a very familiar scene on all the major news networks. As the Lord brought this scene up in my spirit, He told me that "if we (the Church) would pray with the unity of the Muslims, we could stop the black clouds of judgment that were coming to this nation." As I heard the phrase "black clouds of judgment," I understood these clouds to be likened unto sets of waves crashing on the shore. Waves come in sets. There can be five or six waves in a set followed by a lull where there are no waves, but the experienced wave watcher knows that there are more sets of waves to follow.

Let me give a word of clarification about the Muslims in the vision in case someone may misunderstand. The Muslims have a very different doctrine than we Christians do, for they do not even recognize that Jesus Christ is the Son of God. In fact, to say that God had a Son is even considered blasphemy in their faith. We Christians, on the other hand, know that God loved the world so much that "he gave his only begotten Son" (John 3:16), and we also know that Jesus is the only way to the Father (John 14:6). In the vision, the Lord was simply pointing out the dedication of the Muslims to prayer and how they prayed at several times a day with such unity.

We, on the other hand, struggle to get saints together for the evening prayer meeting. Early Morning Prayer is an even harder task! We have to do better than this if we are going to stop the waves of judgment. My friend, based on the word that the Lord gave me, wave two could hit any moment. The good news is that if you and I unite together in prayer, we can stop this judgment and have revival. Let's get busy humbling ourselves and praying so that our land can be healed! Waves of revival beat waves of judgment any day! Our nation is standing at a very crucial point in its history, and quite frankly I don't know if we have fully received our 9-11 wakeup call in order to turn back the remaining waves of judgment. Yet, each new day is another chance from God to make things right. Let's make the most of every opportunity and pray for our land as Nehemiah and Abraham did for theirs. Ultimately, the outcome of this nation rests in the hands of a merciful, yet holy God, but at the same time, we can't sit idly by and do nothing! God's call to prayer is clear. You and I must answer that call and BUILD AGAIN the wall of righteousness that GUARDS THIS LAND as we anticipate His glorious return.

APPENDIX A

YOU MUST BE BORN AGAIN

There was a man of the Pharisees, named Nicodemus, a ruler of the Jews: The same came to Jesus by night, and said unto him, Rabbi, we know that thou art a teacher come from God: for no man can do these miracles that thou doest, except God be with him. Jesus answered and said unto him, Verily, verily, I say unto thee, Except a man be born again, he cannot see the kingdom of God. Nicodemus saith unto him, How can a man be born when he is old? can he enter the second time into his mother's womb, and be born? Jesus answered, Verily, verily, I say unto thee, Except a man be born of water and of the Spirit, he cannot enter into the kingdom of God. John 3:1-5

Jesus said you "must be born again" (John 3:7). He told Nicodemus, a ruler of the Jews, that a man could neither "see the kingdom of God" (John 3:3) nor "enter into the kingdom of God" (John 3:5) unless he was born of water and the Spirit. This spiritual birth from above, we are told, can only come through Jesus Christ. The Gospel of John puts it this way: "But as many as received him (Jesus), to them gave he power to become the sons of God, even to them that believe on his name" (John 1:12). Missing the kingdom of God, i.e. heaven, is far too important of a matter to go through life and leave to chance.

The good news is that you can know for sure where your eternal destination will be! The key to alleviating all doubt is to accept God's record that he has given of his Son or in other words, your Bible. The Apostle John declares: "And this is the record, that God has given to us eternal life, and this life is in his Son. He that hath the Son hath life; and he that hath not the Son of God hath not life." He goes on to say, "These things have I written unto you that believe on the name of the Son of God; that ye MAY KNOW that ye have eternal life" (1 John 5:11-13). Once you accept God's record of his Son, you simply need to do as John 1:12 says and "receive him (Jesus)" so you can now "become a son of God."

You must start by receiving the Son, but you certainly can't stop there! Many people claim to have God as their Father, and some even go so far as to say, "We are all the children of God." Jesus repeatedly claimed that God was his Father, but he was not the only one. The group of Jews he encountered in John chapter 8 claimed to be the seed of Abraham and that God was their Father also. Jesus boldly told them "you are of your father the devil, and the lusts of your father ye will do" (John 8:44). Jesus thus made two groups, those who were "of God" with God as their Father and those who were "of the devil" with devil as their father. What makes the difference? Jesus clarifies, "He that is of God heareth God's words: ye therefore hear them not, because ye are not of God" (John 8:47). So this question of who your father is, spiritually speaking, now boils down to whose words you obey, God's or the devil's. Jesus said that not everyone that says to him "Lord, Lord" will enter the kingdom of heaven, only he that does "the will of my Father which is heaven" (Matt. 7:21).

There will be many, Jesus said, in that day will say to him "Lord, Lord, have we not prophesied in thy name," cast out devils, and done many great things! He goes on to say that on Judgment Day he will profess to them these sobering words: "I never knew you: depart from me, ye that work iniquity" (Matt. 7:22-23). It is not enough just to call Jesus Lord; in order for Jesus truly to be your Lord, you must do what he says.

Do you know for sure that you have eternal life today? Have you received God's Son, Jesus, into your life? Have you truly made Jesus the Lord of your life by obeying him? If not, do not delay any longer! Please join me in a simple prayer like this, asking Jesus Christ into your heart:

Lord Jesus, I believe God's record today that you are the Son of God. I realize that "all have sinned and come short of the glory of God" including me (Rom. 3:23). I believe that you gave your life as "a ransom for many" in order to pay the price for my sins and free me from an eternity with the devil in the Lake of Fire (Mark 10:45). I accept God's gift of eternal life that is only made available through you (Rom. 6:23). I ask you now to forgive me of my sins and come into my heart as my Lord and Savior. With the help of the Holy Spirit, I will live for you the rest of my days. In Your name, Amen!

APPENDIX B

HAVE YOU RECEIVED THE HOLY GHOST SINCE YOU BELIEVED?

And it came to pass, that, while Apollos was at Corinth, Paul having passed through the upper coasts came to Ephesus: and finding certain disciples, He said unto them, Have ye received the Holy Ghost since ye believed? Acts 19:1-2a

Paul obviously thought this was a very important question to this group of disciples in Ephesus that he found on his missionary journey that day (Acts 19:2). If it was so important to that group of disciples, then it certainly is still an important question for believers today. This particular group of disciples had not yet heard of Jesus, for they were only baptized unto John's baptism of repentance. Paul informed them of the rest of John's message: "they should believe on him which should come after him, that is, on Jesus" (Acts 19:4). After they received his message of Christ, Paul "laid hands on them, the Holy Ghost came on them; and they spake with tongues and prophesied" (Acts 19:6).

When Peter was called upon by the Lord Jesus to go and preach the gospel to Cornelius and his house, he did so only after he had his believing corrected by the Master. While he

APPENDIX

was delivering his awesome message to Cornelius and his household, he was interrupted by the Holy Spirit falling upon his audience that received the word (Acts 10:44). Later, back at Jerusalem, he had a hard sale trying to convince those that were of the circumcision. He rehearsed the whole matter for them from start to finish (Acts 11:2-4). The argument that he used to convince his contenders was that "the Holy Ghost fell on them, as on us at the beginning." Peter said he then remembered what Jesus had said, "John indeed baptized with water; but ye shall be baptized with the Holy Ghost." He concluded, "God gave them the like gift as did unto us who believed on the Lord Jesus Christ; what was I that I could withstand God?" After that sale, his contenders glorified God and agreed God had also granted the Gentiles "repentance unto life" (Acts 11:15-18). Given this major development for the Church that day with the gospel being preached to the Gentiles for the first time, I would also have to conclude that receiving the Holy Ghost after believing is very important matter!

When the gift of the Holy Ghost was given to them at the beginning, "they were all filled with the Holy Ghost, and began to speak with other tongues as the Spirit gave them utterance" (Acts 2:4). In Peter's sermon on the day of Pentecost, he was asked a question of those who were convicted of their sin of crucifying the Lord Jesus, "what shall we do?" He replied, "Repent and be baptized every one of you in the name of Jesus Christ for the remission of sins, and ye shall receive the gift of the Holy Ghost." Then he made clear for his audience that day and for those of us who have since believed concerning the gift of the Holy Ghost, "For the promise is unto you, and to your children, and to all that are afar off, even as many as the Lord our God shall call" (Acts 2:38-39).

If the Holy Ghost has not yet fell upon you since you have believed, receive the promise of the Holy Ghost today by faith. Recognize that Jesus is the one who baptizes with the Holy Ghost. Then, ask Him today to baptize you with the precious Holy Ghost with the evidence of speaking in other tongues. "After that the Holy Ghost is come upon you," the Bible says, you will receive God's power from on high to be a mighty witness (Acts 1:8). Once you have received the Baptism of the Holy Ghost, go out and tell the good news of Jesus Christ with boldness and power!

APPENDIX

About the Author:

Kent Evans is the Sr. Pastor of Faith Harvest International Church (Richmond, VA) along with his lovely wife and co-pastor Martha. Pastor Kent answered the call to preach the gospel over twenty-five years ago and has served in various roles in ministry since then. Recently, Pastor Kent received his Masters of Divinity from Liberty University with a concentration in Evangelism and Church Growth. Pastor Kent has a passion to see believers get an understanding of the Word of God, so that the devil will no longer be able to steal from them what God has promised. At Faith Harvest, Pastor Kent continues to stress the importance of the principles of love, unity, and prayer contained in this book in order that the people of God may "work together in love to reap the end-time harvest by faith."

Other books from the Author:

Keeping Yourself in the Love of God
Available at Amazon.com

For more information please contact:

Appointed Time Ministries
121 Wyck St.
Suite 301
Richmond, VA 23225

Website: www.yourappointedtime.org
Email: pastork@yourappointedtime.org

www.ingramcontent.com/pod-product-compliance
Lightning Source LLC
Chambersburg PA
CBHW070545030426
42337CB00016B/2351